What it's Like To Build a House: *The Diary of a Builder*

What it's Like To Build a House: *The Diary of a Builder*

Bob Syvanen

The Taunton Press

All drawings by Bob Syvanen
Photos by Bob Syvanen

First printing: August 1985
International Standard Book Number: 0-918804-41-8
Library of Congress Catalog Card Number: 85-50839
Printed in the United States of America

A FINE HOMEBUILDING Book

FINE HOMEBUILDING® is a trademark of
The Taunton Press, Inc.,
registered in the U.S. Patent and Trademark Office.

The Taunton Press, Inc.
63 South Main Street
Box 355
Newtown, Connecticut 06470

Acknowledgments

This book is dedicated to my wife, Pat, whose love and joy in life are a constant inspiration to me. This book is also dedicated to my now-grown children, Robert, Liisie, Richard and Ginger. I love them all.

I thank those who involved themselves in this building project: Betty, Fritz, Bruce, John, Ed, Doug, Richard, Charles and all the subs. They built the house.

Introduction

This is a book of design and construction tips and tricks. They are based on a specific house, but this is not a book on how to build that house. Instead it's a daily log of the job, with emphasis on the highlights, both good and bad. The tips and tricks I've included are the kinds of things that crop up on a job here and a job there, and get stored away for later use. For every problem there is always a solution, and the quicker that solution surfaces, the less costly the problem is—time is money.

The project started at a local beach party on Cape Cod when my friend Betty Price asked me about a solar house I had been working on. To make a long story short (that's my style), in mid-December I agreed to design and build a house for Betty on a lot she had just bought.

Betty wanted a house that looked like a traditional Cape Cod, but that would use an active solar system. I tried, but the first design I came up with would have been too expensive to build. So we agreed to simplify the design. The living room, kitchen, one bedroom and a bathroom are on the lower level, and the garage, storage area, sewing room and another bedroom and bath are on the upper level. (The upper level is road level.) The concrete garage floor is the ceiling of the bedroom below, which meant that the slab would have to have a lot of steel in it. Sometimes when you simplify, you complicate. The roof would start about a foot above grade on the high side of the sloped lot. By using a wood-shingled hip roof, I was hoping that I could minimize the house visually.

The house design took shape quickly, and after a few modifications, such as changing the roof from a hip to a gable end (for more usable floor space) and changing the dog-house dormers at the garage and entry to shed dormers, we were ready to start building.

The ingredients that go into fast, smooth housebuilding are a flat lot, standard, simple design, experienced and reliable help, and confidence. I have designed and built many houses, but this one was to be the most interesting and the most challenging. I had the confidence, but the design, although simple, is not standard by any means. The lot sloped and the help was strictly 9 to 5. Consequently, the house took more time to build than it should have.

Dec. 29

I've built on sloping lots before, so I knew there were problems that would have to be worked out with the foundation and drainage. But what I didn't realize was that the 100-yd.-wide and 2-ft.-deep pond at one end of the property was considered "wetlands." This put it in the conservationist's realm, and approval by the conservation commission was required before a house could be built on the property.

The site, and its "wetlands" pond.

A perk test is a must to evaluate the soil condition for the septic system. There must be no ground water in the test holes, and the soil should not restrict drainage. In the case of this lot, the 13-ft.- and 14-ft.-deep test holes showed sandy soil and no ground water.

Jan. 2

I attack house design like any other project—start something, even if it's foolish.

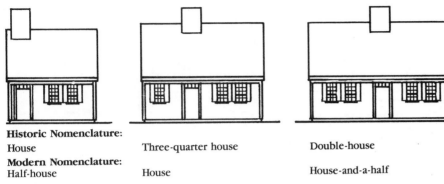

Historic Nomenclature:
House

Modern Nomenclature:
Half-house

Three-quarter house

House

Double-house

House-and-a-half

The owner wanted a traditional Cape Cod house, but solar-heated, on her south-facing lot. The first design I came up with was a Cape Cod half-house with an attached garage. Betty and her son Charlie worked the sketches over and settled on what they wanted, and I went on from there.

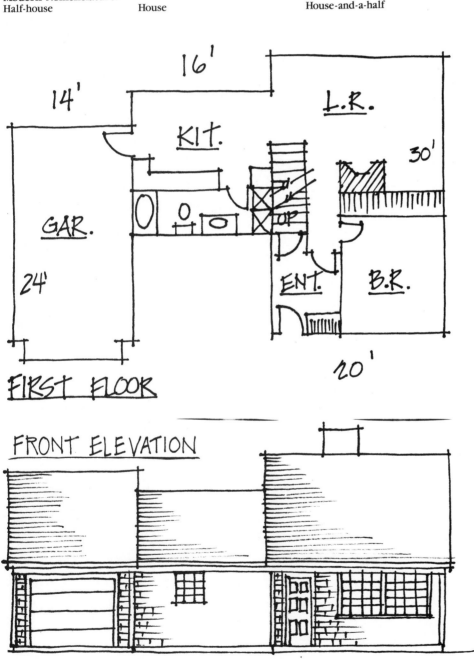

FIRST FLOOR

FRONT ELEVATION

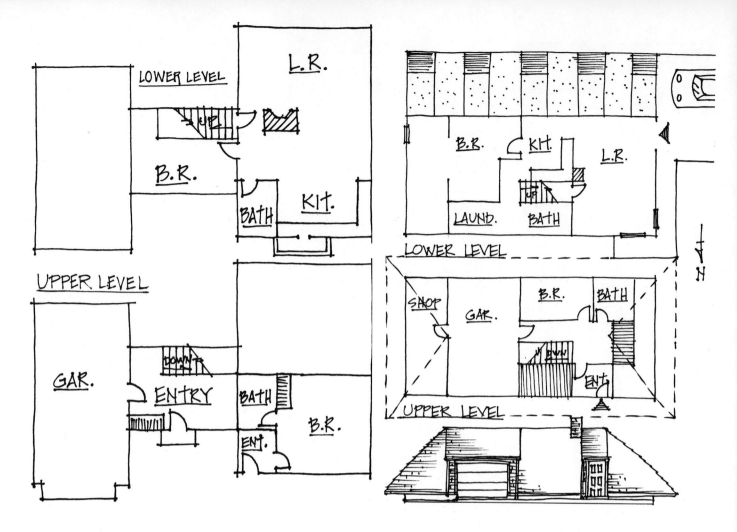

The revised floor plan, shown in the drawing at above left, has the living room on the lower level. Not a bad plan, but all the jogs in the exterior walls would have made the foundation difficult and expensive to form.

To cut costs, I went to a rectangular shape and tucked the house into the hillside, as shown in the drawing at above right. Not bad.

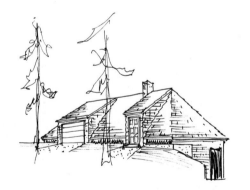

A quick perspective gives the feel.

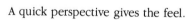

The end elevation shows the relationship between road, house and slope.

This is the final floor plan. We decided that the upper level would be for guests and would have an air-lock entry. (The reinforced-concrete garage slab is also on this level.) The main living area would be on the lower level.

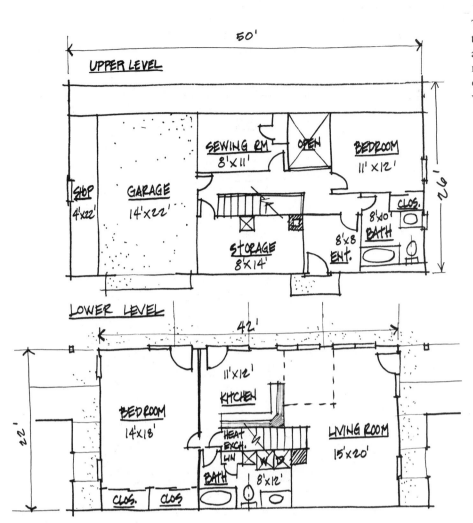

UPPER LEVEL

50'

26'

SHOP
4'x22'

GARAGE
14'x22'

SEWING RM
8'x11'

OPEN

BEDROOM
11'x12'

STORAGE
8'x14'

8'x8
ENT.

BATH
8'x10'

CLOS.

LOWER LEVEL

42'

22'

BEDROOM
14x18'

KITCHEN
11'x12'

HEAT
EXCH.
LIN.

BATH
8'x12'

CLOS.

CLOS

LIVING ROOM
15'x20'

Some quickie elevations, done on graph paper, and we are almost there.

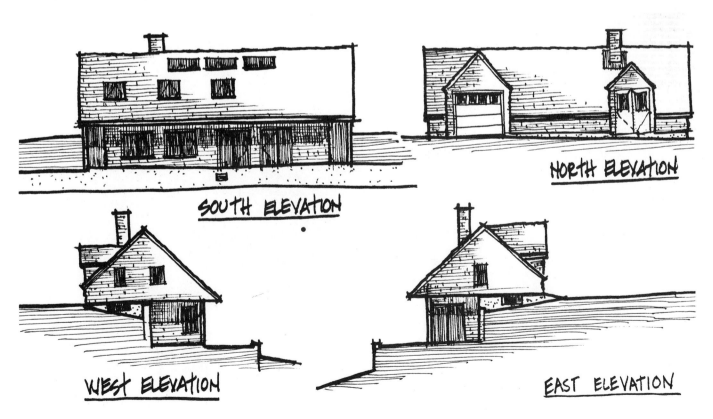

SOUTH ELEVATION

NORTH ELEVATION

WEST ELEVATION

EAST ELEVATION

5

This perspective gives the feel of it, but something is wrong. The shed dormers over the entry and garage, replacing the dog-house dormers, clean up the front.

A perspective looking from the southwest, and the house feels right. After 28 hours of sketching and talking, we were ready to start the working plans.

Feb. 5

The working plans are shown below and on the following page. It took me 42 hours to draw them.

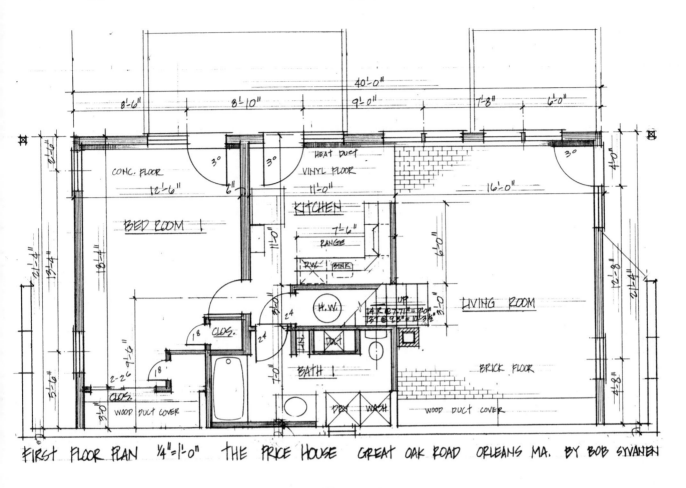

FIRST FLOOR PLAN ¼"=1'-0" THE PRICE HOUSE GREAT OAK ROAD ORLEANS MA. BY BOB SYVANEN

The heart of this house is the active solar heating system, and much of the design and construction relates to it. The system was not to be the sole source of heat but was to join forces with a wood stove, passive solar gain and backup radiant heat in the ceiling. (The backup radiant heat consists of heating elements in a plastic sheet and was to be used when all else failed.) Heat loss is kept to a minimum by putting most of the north side of the house in the ground and by insulating the house well. Passive solar gain is achieved through large south-facing windows: Brick and concrete floors soak up the sunlight during the day, releasing it as heat at night.

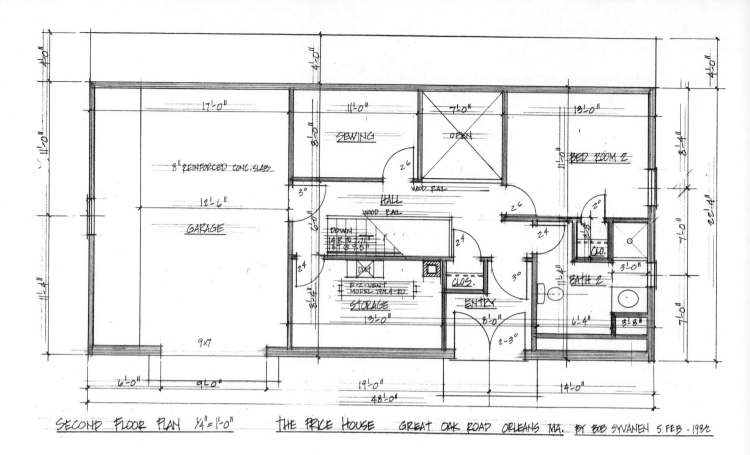

SECOND FLOOR PLAN ¼"=1'-0"   THE PRICE HOUSE   GREAT OAK ROAD   ORLEANS MA.   BY BOB SYVANEN 5.FEB.1982

The active solar gain is in the form of hot air circulated from an attic heatbox that has a south-facing skylight, as shown on the facing page. The low-speed fan that circulates the hot air is automatically turned on when the heatbox temperature reaches 90⁰. The air travels down an insulated duct to a covered trench in the floor along the north wall on the lower level. A similar trench, but with an open grill cover, runs along the south wall on the lower level. The north and south trenches are connected by 3-in.-diameter PVC pipes at 12 in. on center in the concrete and brick floors, as shown at right. The air in the north "header" trench goes through the PVC pipes into the south "exhaust" trench, then up through the open grillwork in the living room, kitchen and bedroom. To complete the circulation loop, the air re-enters the heatbox through two grills in the ceiling on the upper level.

Heating Ductwork in Concrete Slab

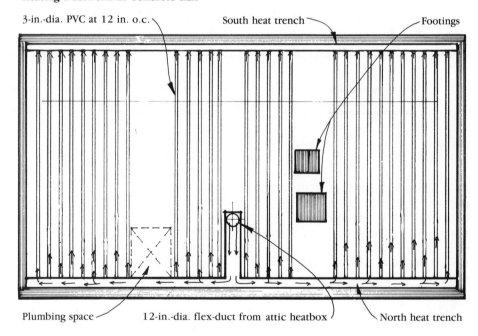

3-in.-dia. PVC at 12 in. o.c.   South heat trench   Footings

Plumbing space   12-in.-dia. flex-duct from attic heatbox   North heat trench

Active-Solar Heat-Flow Schematic

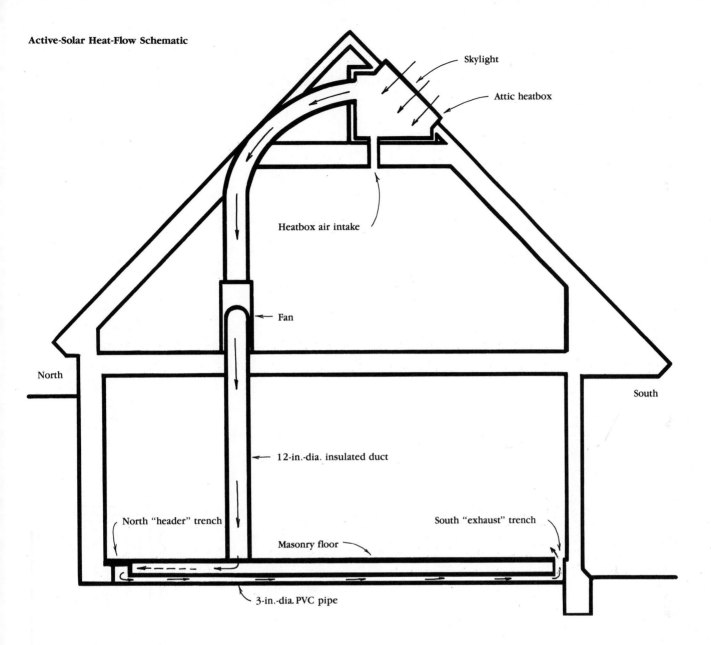

Skylight

Attic heatbox

Heatbox air intake

Fan

North

South

12-in.-dia. insulated duct

North "header" trench

South "exhaust" trench

Masonry floor

3-in.-dia. PVC pipe

I had plastic jugs filled with water in the heatbox to store the heat, but one of the jugs failed and it had to be removed. The jugs were not made for this purpose, and though I was assured that they would work, I did not trust the other jugs and so removed them all. We could have used containers especially made for heat storage, but cost was a factor at the time of construction. This coming winter we are going to try the system with no jugs—just air.

A tight house must have clean air, so installing a heat exchanger, although costly, was necessary. A heat exchanger takes in outside air while exhausting inside air and in the process transfers the heat from the warm inside air to the cold incoming air.

A sloped lot always presents a problem for concrete footings. To get below the frost line, the footing on the low side has to be lower than the footing on the high side—you have to get the high-side footing to tie in with the low-side footing. I designed the foundation scheme shown at right, but I did not get it. My foundation design would use more concrete, but all footing bottoms would be below the frost line. The outside faces of the 10-in.-thick east and west frost walls would line up with the outside faces of the exterior living-room and bedroom stud walls, and could be easily insulated on the outside with 2-in.-thick foam. What I got instead, shown at below right, were 16-in.-wide footings under the east and west stud walls that had to be cut in order to align them with the living-room and bedroom stud walls (p. 19).

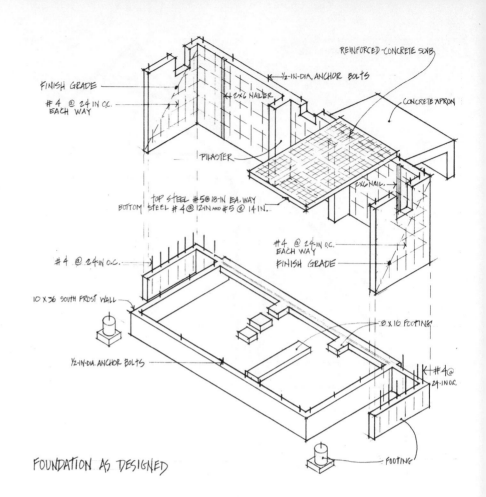

FOUNDATION AS DESIGNED

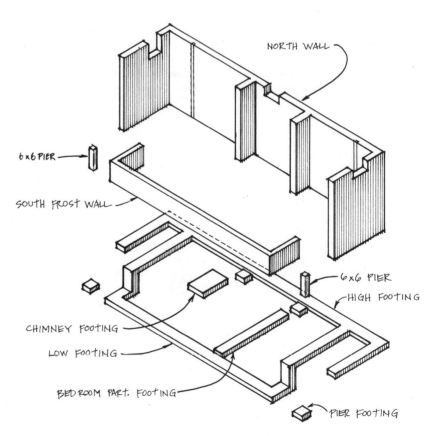

FOUNDATION AS BUILT

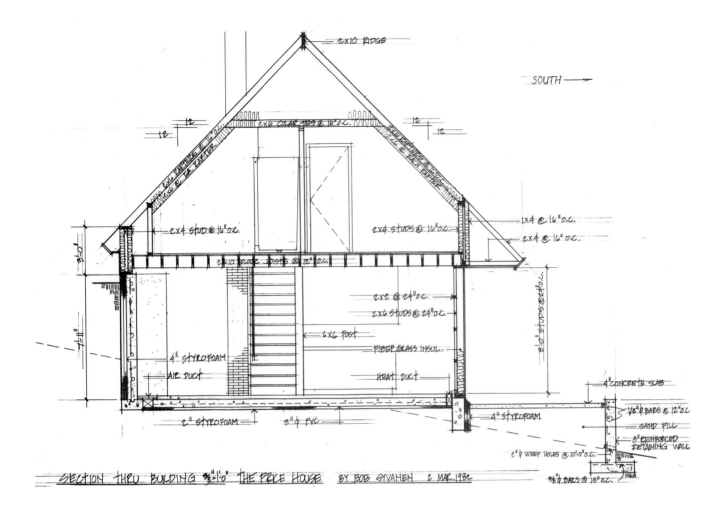

SECTION THRU BUILDING 3⁄8"=1'-0" THE PRICE HOUSE   BY BOB SYVANEN   2 MAR. 1982

The original house design called for two sets of 6-ft.-wide by full-length glass patio-door units and two 6-ft.-wide by 4-ft.-high window units on the south wall. To shade the glass from summer sun, I designed a 4-ft. overhang on the south roof, which you can see in the drawing above.

After more design revisions, the patio doors were reduced to 3-ft.-wide by full-length units flanked by 3-ft.-wide by 4-ft. high windows. When the rafters were installed in April, it was apparent from the shadow line on the south wall that the house would not really benefit from the spring and fall sun, as the only sun that would get in the house would be through the lower section of the two glass doors. To overcome this, I decided to leave sections of the roof and soffit open above the windows and doors. These openings, which I call sunholes, are designed to allow fall and spring sun in and still shade the house from summer sun.

SOUTH ELEVATION ⅛"=1'-0"

EAST ELEVATION ⅛"=1'-0"

11

This is the roof-framing plan—nothing unusual here.

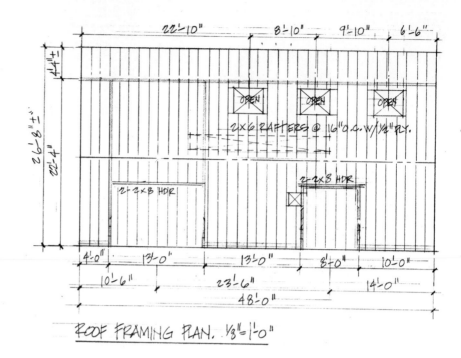

ROOF FRAMING PLAN. ⅛"=1'-0"

There's nothing unusual in the floor-framing plan either.

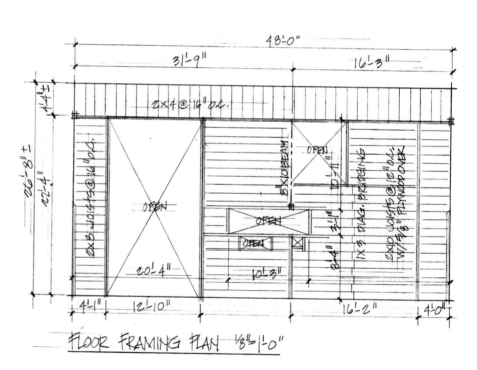

FLOOR FRAMING PLAN ⅛"=1'-0"

Mar. 4

Made a lumber list and gave a copy to three lumberyards. Checked window and skylight prices at the lumberyards to compare them with prices at a yard that specializes in doors and windows. The lumberyards were high. Got the fire-alarm permit from the firehouse and the septic plan from the engineer so that I could get the building permit from town hall.

PRICE HOUSE 3 MAR. 82 (BOB SYVANEN)				
ALL FRAMING TO BE KD				
SILLS-PRESSURE-TREATED	2x4	3/16'		
	2x6	2/10'	2/12'	3/14'
	2x8	2/14'		
	2x10	4/12'		
FLOOR JOISTS-	2x10	26/12'	28/16'	
	2x8	14/12'		
BEAM-	8x10	1/12'		
BRIDGING-	1x3	100 L.F.		
STUDS-P HDRS & SILLS	2x6	70/8'	6/10'	16/12'	6/14'
	2x4	200/8'	5/10'	75/12'	12/14'
POST	6x6	3/10'		
FURRING	2x2	40/12'		
RAFTERS	2x6	38/18'	39/16'	
	2x4	12/10'	5/12'	
TIES	2x6	33/12'		
RIDGE	2x10	2/12'	1/14'	
	2x8	1/14'		
	2x6	1/12'		

SOFFIT BLK-	2x12	2/10'	
STAIR STRINGERS- (CARRIAGES)	2x12	3/14'	
TREADS-OAK-	9½"x36"- 13		
RISERS ("D"SELECT)-1x10	4/12'		
SUBFLOOR-	5/8 PLYSCORE	32 SH	
UNDERLAY-	5/8"	10 SH	
SHEATHING-ROOF-		66 SH	
" WALL-		32 SH	
EXTER. TRIM- RAKE & FASCIA-	1x10	6/10' 6/12' 2/14' 2/16'	
ROUGH CEDAR	1x4	6/10' 6/12' 2/14' 2/16'	
CORNER BOARDS-	5/4x6	1/12'	
ROUGH CEDAR	5/4x5	1/12'	
SOFFIT-	1x6	400 SQ. FT.	
ROUGH CEDAR- SHIPLAP-			
DOORS-EXT.- 3- 3'-0"+3'-0" FIX.GL. INSWING W/INSUL.GL.			
2- 3'-0' DOUBLE ENT. W/GL. EA. DR. M-136			
DOORS-INT.- 1- 3'-0" SOLID CORE			
(RAISED PANEL) 1- 3'-0" W/GLASS (INSUL.)			
2- 3'-0" W/SLIDING HDWRE			
1- 2'-0"			
5- 2'-4"			

DOORS-INT- 3- 2'-6"	
(CONT.) 2- 1'-6"	
GARAGE- OVERHEAD -w/GLASS- 7'x9'	
WINDOWS- PELLA WOOD CASEMENT	
2- 2448 WC 2	
3- 2448 WC	
2- 2440 WC	
1- 1636 WC	
SKYLIGHTS- ROTO- 3- W4141	
WOOD LOUVERS- 2- B-2807	
WHITE CEDAR SHINGLES- 10 SQ.	
RED CEDAR SHINGLES - 20 SQ.	
15# FELT - 6 ROLLS	
NAILS- 50#- 16d COM. GALV.	
" 10d " "	
" 8d " "	
" 6d " "	
" 1⅛" WOOD SHINGLE NAILS	
12" ZINC - 1 ROLL	
2" STYROFOAM- 4x8 - 51 SH	
3"Ø THINWALL PVC - 68/10'-0"	

This is my original lumber list. The list doesn't have to be fancy, nor does it have to be accurate to the last 2x4. I have never built a house that didn't require more lumber—2x4s are the most commonly reordered stock. To make up a lumber list, I work from the plans, starting with the mud sills and ending with hardware. The material is broken down into lumber dimensions, quantity and length: "2x4 $3/16$' " means three 16-ft. 2x4s.

Permits—it used to be a sketch and a few dollars were all you needed. Now you need a permit for the building, the fire alarm, the septic system, town water and electrical and plumbing systems, and each one has a fee.

For the building permit, you need at least one full set of plans, which usually includes floor plans, a section through the building and a plot plan. The plot plan shows the location of the house relative to the lot lines and road. Some towns require more than one set of plans and even require that an engineer stake out the foundation.

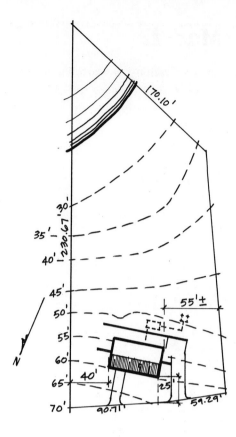

Mar. 5

Set corner stakes for the excavator, and contacted the electrician to set the work pole.

I used 5-ft. lengths of ⅝-in. rebar and set the side lines 15⁰ to the west of north/south to keep the front and back walls parallel to the sloping lot.

Mar. 12

The excavation was started and I checked it out. I wanted to make sure that the hole was in the right place. I located the work-pole spot for the electrician.

Mar. 15

Excavation finished.

Mar. 16

Set corner stakes for footings.

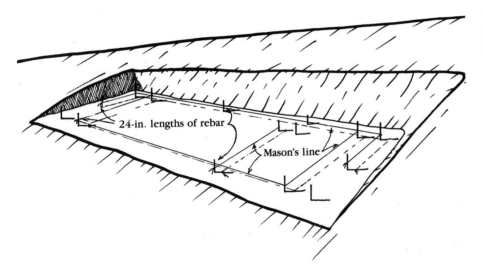

24-in. lengths of rebar

Mason's line

For locating corners of the foundation, 24-in. lengths of ½-in. rebar make good stakes. Don't drive stakes in solidly until all corners are located and squared properly. Mason's line connecting the stakes outlines the foundation. I haven't seen batter boards used in years.

Footing forms are in and I check the work.

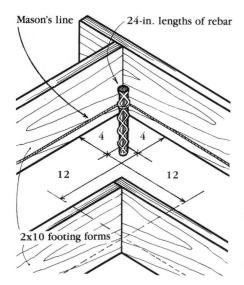

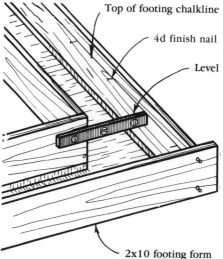

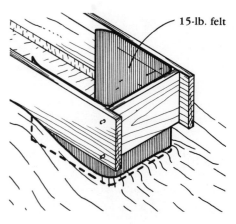

A piece of 15-lb. felt, stapled to the inside face of a footing form that is open on the bottom, will contain the concrete. I saw it work.

The 2x10 footing forms are offset 4 in. outside the string and 12 in. inside the string, as shown above. The 16-in.-wide footing will support an 8-in.-thick concrete foundation wall.

A good excavator can give you a level floor to within an inch or two of the bottom of the footings. The footing forms are set on this grade. They don't have to be level, outside corners can run by and inside boards can lap. A chalkline is snapped to show the top of the footings, and the trench is dug to the depth required. The amount of digging is usually that inch or two left by the excavator. If the excavator dug a little deep anyplace don't fill it in, or the dirt will settle later and cause the footing to crack. It is better to leave the footing a little thicker in those places.

For the chalkline, shoot the top of the footing with a transit and mark it on the inside of each outside corner. Snap a chalkline (red is best) to connect the corners. Drive in 4d finish nails on the line at about 24 in. on center—these nails make it easy to level the concrete. Locate the line on the opposite form by leveling over.

Mar. 22

Footings are poured.

The footings are ready for the foundation walls.

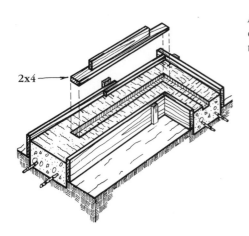

2x4

A 2x4 keyway for the foundation walls can be pressed into the footings after the concrete has stiffened a bit.

Mar. 23

Wall forms are up and I check the work.

Mar. 25

Wall forms are stripped, and all is well.

The foundation is ready for insulation.

Mar. 29

I check and compare lumberyard prices. There's not much difference in price, so I choose my favorite yard and order material for sills, some studs (2x6x8'), 2-in.-thick rigid foam insulation and metal lath for the foundation walls. I also order a mess of 2x4s and 2x6s, and 8d, 10d, and 16d common galvanized nails.

Mar. 30

Cut the footings to correct error. Laid out and drilled sills. Finished the sills and started securing the 2x4 nailers to the foundation walls. (All the sills and nailers are pressure-treated.)

I wanted the outside faces of the east and west exterior walls to line up with the outside faces of the footing, so I could insulate the outside of the foundation, as shown at right. The foundation man gave me a wide footing that I could insulate, but the footing would show past the walls after the insulation was beveled, as shown at far right. Cutting the footing with a gasoline-powered concrete-cutting saw worked okay, but it took three hours and three cutting disks to make a 4-in.-deep cut 22 ft. long.

Drilling through a 2x4 nailer into the concrete with a combination drill-hammer, shown at bottom right, makes easy work of a difficult job. A piece of tape wrapped around the bit at 3⅛ in. from the tip makes a simple depth guide.

At bottom far right, a 3-in.-long #14 flat-head wood screw, with a #14-16 plastic anchor screwed a few turns onto the tip, carefully driven into the hole until the plastic anchor is at the bottom of the hole, will leave an inch of wood screw to screw home.

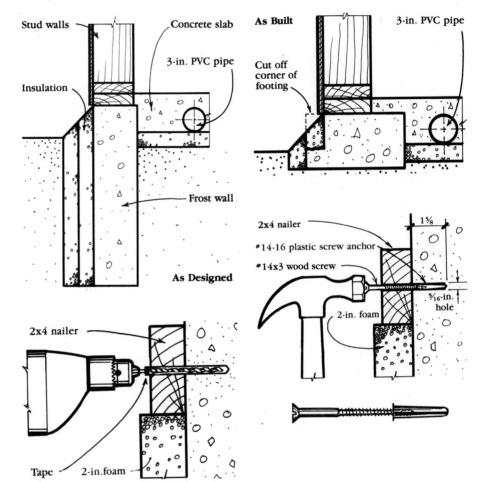

Stud walls · Concrete slab · As Built · 3-in. PVC pipe

3-in. PVC pipe

Insulation · Cut off corner of footing

Frost wall

As Designed

2x4 nailer · 1⅝

#14-16 plastic screw anchor

#14x3 wood screw

2-in. foam · ⁵⁄₁₆-in. hole

2x4 nailer

Tape · 2-in. foam

19

Mar. 31

Finished horizontal nailers. Set all the sills in place temporarily and checked for level. Started shimming and mortaring sills and installing foam insulation. The north wall is waterproofed with Karnak 920.

When checking the foundation walls before installing the sills, I found the northwest corner 1 in. high...

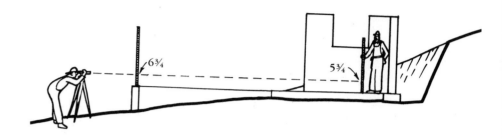

...So I had to taper the bottom of the sill. A few cuts to the depth of the taper with a handsaw followed by a sharp hatchet made quick work of tapering.

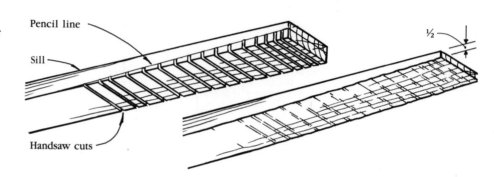

To level sills, I use a 2-in. by 2-in. wood shim at each anchor bolt. Each shim is custom-measured for the thickness necessary to bring the sill to level by shooting the elevation at each bolt with a transit. I lay in my mortar a little thicker than the shim, so that the sill, when squeezed down, will be on a solid bed. The mix must be soupy, and the foundation top wet down.

I have also leveled the sills after the joists and deck are in place. I raise the sill with a flat bar, then slip wood-shingle tips, slate or stones under the sill. The shims, at about 24 in. on center, should be back from the outer edge of the sill to make room for the mortar, which is then forced into the resulting space. This only works if there is access to the inside of the foundation wall; a crawl space would be a tough place to mortar from.

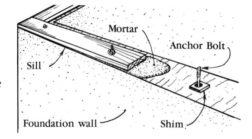

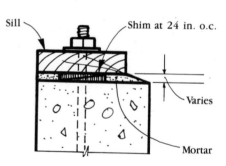

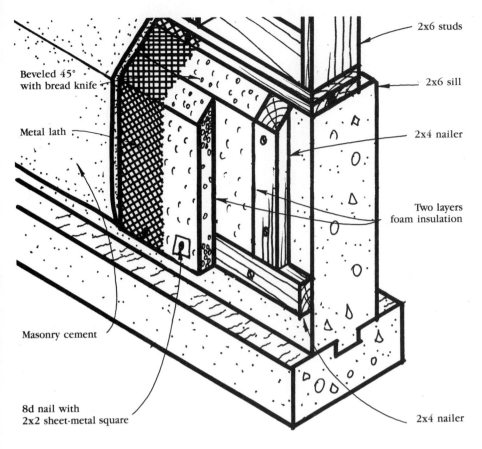

Beveled 45° with bread knife

Metal lath

Masonry cement

8d nail with 2x2 sheet-metal square

2x6 studs

2x6 sill

2x4 nailer

Two layers foam insulation

2x4 nailer

The outside faces of the foundation walls are covered with two layers of 2-in.-thick foam insulation, as shown at left. The first layer has 2x4 pressure-treated nailers 24 in. on center for the second layer of foam to nail to.

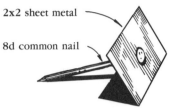

2x2 sheet metal

8d common nail

Aluminum or zinc 2-in. by 2-in. sheet-metal squares with an 8d common nail through the center secure the foam to the nailers.

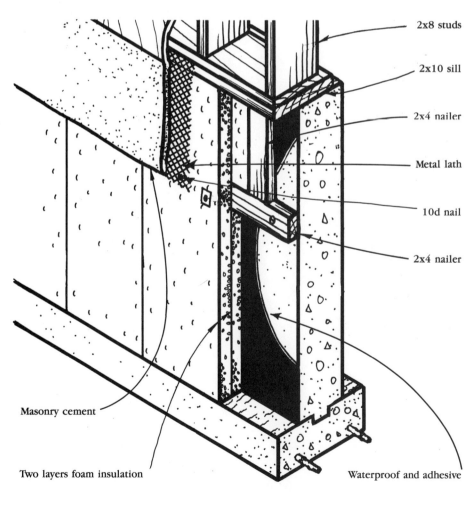

2x8 studs

2x10 sill

2x4 nailer

Metal lath

10d nail

2x4 nailer

Masonry cement

Two layers foam insulation

Waterproof and adhesive

The high north wall has a troweled-on layer of waterproofing adhesive, which is compatible with foam.

I didn't use a termite shield in this house, but I could have if I had come up with this solution sooner.

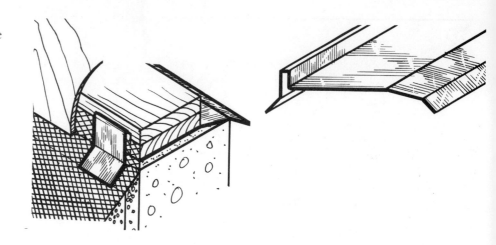

Apr. 2

Ran out of the waterproofing, and the only place this stuff is available is three hours away. As luck would have it, a friend who had just bought two cans of it stopped by. Needless to say, I quickly talked him out of one of those cans. My daughter Liisie and a helper finished waterproofing and insulating the north wall.

Apr. 3

Finished mortaring sills and laying up foam insulation, but I was four pieces short. A check with the lumberyard revealed that they had run out, so it was back-ordered. Started to shape the foam, beveling it 45° with a breadknife, and to install the metal lath.

Apr. 5

Finished metal lath on foundation walls. Town water was to go in today, but no show. Can't backfill until the water pipes are in under the footing.

The north wall has Karnak waterproofing, foam insulation and 2x4 pressure-treated nailers. A second layer of insulation goes over this one, followed by metal lath over the upper 2 ft.

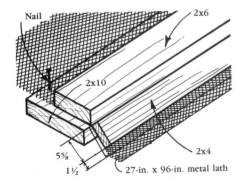

Pre-bending metal lath to fit the wall surface is the best way to get a good fit.

The south wall has foam insulation and metal lath.

Apr. 6

Snow today, schools closed. I guess that is why town water didn't show.

Apr. 7

Terrific blizzard today. Town water was a no show again.

Apr. 8

Backfill started just as town water showed up.

Apr. 10

Picked up my radial-saw stand at the welder's. It was there a month waiting to be repaired and painted. I settled for a quick weld job: I couldn't wait any longer.

Apr. 12

Set the radial saw in place and built the lower-level exterior walls. I am working alone. There are many visitors asking questions about this unusual house.

Unless a wide table is required, a 2x10 wing on each end of the radial-saw table is adequate for most work. A straight 2x4 on edge for a guide, backed up with another 2x4, makes a good, strong setup.

On this job I had a problem because the wings were not long enough to accommodate the 20-ft.-long joists. The solution was to nail an extension to the 2x4 guide. The 1x3 stop out in space worked well because it never collected sawdust—sawdust against the stop causes errors when duplicating parts.

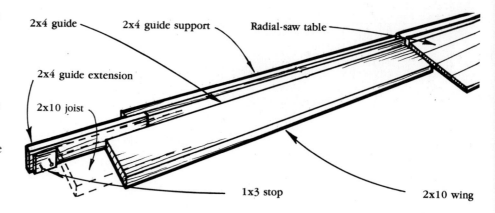

Apr. 13

Electrician set work pole. Finished lower-level partitions and started the 4-ft.-high, 2x8 north wall. The excavator came by with a bill—800 yards of fill at $3.00 per yard. Dirt is not dirt-cheap anymore. One of the problems with a sloped lot is the need for fill.

Most electricians have work poles all rigged up. I like to have a 220V outlet that requires a special adapter. This prevents anyone from accidentally plugging in a 110V tool.

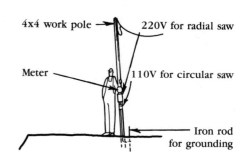

Apr. 15

Sheathed lower bearing walls with ⅝-in. plywood, other exterior walls with ½-in. plywood. Forgot about the heat trench in the floor of the south side of the building, so had to cut and frame for it. Wrapped the bottom of the interior bearing partition that will be buried in the floor slab with aluminum to keep the concrete away from the wood. Finished the short north wall. Started laying out posts to support joist beams.

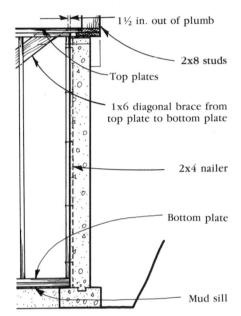

- 1½ in. out of plumb
- 2x8 studs
- Top plates
- 1x6 diagonal brace from top plate to bottom plate
- 2x4 nailer
- Bottom plate
- Mud sill

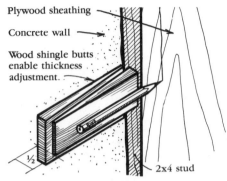

- Plywood sheathing
- Concrete wall
- Wood shingle butts enable thickness adjustment.
- ½
- 2x4 stud

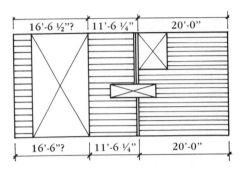

16'-6 ½"?   11'-6 ¼"   20'-0"

16'-6"?   11'-6 ¼"   20'-0"

I cut the top plates of the lower-level walls 1½ in. longer than the bottom plates to compensate for the north foundation wall, which was 1½ in. out of plumb. I never assume any work others do is plumb or square. I always double-check my own work, too. Two lower-level partitions that will support the reinforced-concrete slab above have a let-in 1x6 diagonal brace and ⅝-in. plywood sheathing.

The plywood sheathing against the concrete wall had to be scribed to fit, but I had no compass. So I slid two pieces of wood shingle butt, with a pencil held against the face of the plywood, on the surface of the concrete wall.

The lower-level framing dimensions worked out to be 40 ft. ⅛ in. on the south wall and 40 ft. ¼ in. on the north wall—not bad. When it came to framing the floor, ½ in. extra appeared on the south side. I checked, double-checked and triple-checked, but could not find where I went wrong. The job must go on so I let it go, but this ½ in. was to follow me into the rafters.

Apr. 16

Somehow I was missing one 20-ft.-long and one 18-ft.-long 2x10, which required a trip to the lumberyard. Finished floor joists except for the 4-ft.-long joists in the garage. Friday is cleanup day. I like to start a new week with a clean job site.

Apr. 17

Home work today. Ordered rafter material and sheathing. Worked out details for rafters and dormers, and sunholes in the south-roof overhang.

The sunholes allow more fall and spring sun to come through the windows and doors than would a solid roof. There is still enough overhang at the holes to shade the summer sun.

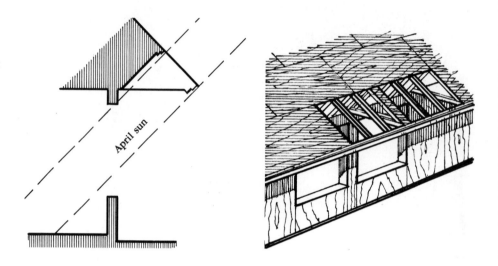

April sun

The horizontal 2x4s in the soffit over the windows and doors in the south overhang are left out because of the sunholes.

The overhang allows fall sun through the windows, as shown, while shading them from most midsummer sun.

Apr. 19

Finished floor joists and decking. South knee wall up, garage and entrance north walls framed. Laid out the rafters, in pencil, on the deck. More visitors.

Apr. 20

Checked all work for square and plumb. Straightened and braced walls. Built movable staging for rafter work. Finished just as the lumber truck drove up with rafter material at 10:00 a.m. I have two men working with me on this job, but one showed up at noon with tendonitis in both elbows. I think he is finished. My other man went home to get a friend of his who just left another job. I put him right to work. Cut most of the rafters and put up quite a few. The boys forgot to allow for skylights and chimney. The plumber came by to talk about getting the pipes in before the concrete slab. He will start Monday, he says.

This movable staging holds a section of ridge in the upper cradles. The cradles are ½ in. short so that the ridge can be shimmed up. The staging is moved to support the next ridge section after the first section has been installed.

The staging planks are set at a height that makes nailing the rafters in place a comfortable job.

Apr. 21

Left the house at 7:00 a.m. to get things ready for the boys. The new guy didn't show until 8:15 a.m., and the other guy didn't show at all. Sent the new guy to find his friend, and by the time we got things together, it was 10:00 a.m. Reframed around skylights and started the garage and entry roofs.

Rafters frame around garage and entry dormers on the north wall.

Main rafters and dormers complete with rafter-tail blocking (p. 33) in place.

Apr. 22

Had an emergency call for a gutter repair job. Worked until 10:00 a.m. cutting rafters and headers to line up work for the boys to do while I was gone.

Haste makes waste. A length of 106½ in. was marked on the guide, and a 1x3 stop was nailed on. But the rafter stock had to be shimmed out 3½ in. for the sawblade to be clear, which caused the rafter to be cut 1 in. short. I usually measure the first piece that is cut, but in my haste to line up work I blew it. A 1-in. strip nailed on the rafter end made it right.

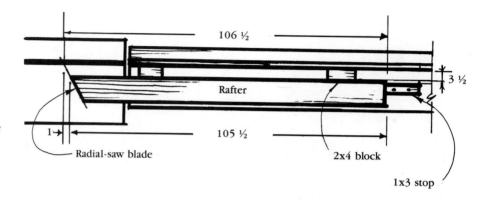

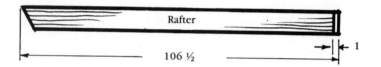

Apr. 23

Everyone was on time today. We put in a pair of gable rafters to support the last 2x10 ridge board. I thought the ridge would be low, but it was 2 in. high. I checked building widths, plumb ends, rafter lengths, everything I could think of. And everything checked out. I finally checked the birdsmouth cut and there the error was: The guy who cut it, blew it. The cut was 1½ in. off. Had we picked any other rafter, things would have been fine. The defective rafter would have showed up later.

This plywood-marking jig should have made locating the birdsmouth on the rafter tail foolproof, but through careless positioning, a birdsmouth was located in the wrong place.

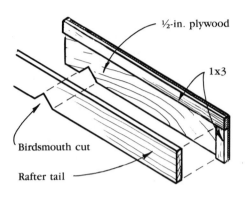

½-in. plywood

1x3

Birdsmouth cut

Rafter tail

Apr. 24

Finished rafters.

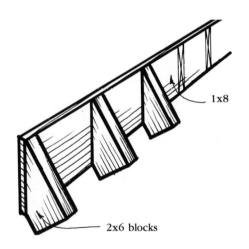

1x8

2x6 blocks

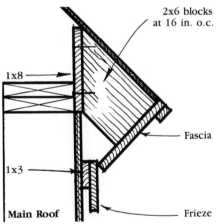

2x6 blocks at 16 in. o.c.

1x8

1x3

Main Roof

Fascia

Frieze

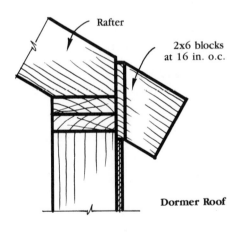

Rafter

2x6 blocks at 16 in. o.c.

Dormer Roof

I like the system for rafter tails shown in the drawings above, because it ensures that all tails will be the same size and in perfect alignment. I cut all the tail blocks from rafter scraps. The blocks are nailed to a 1x8 or plywood. Each one of these 8-ft.-long to 12-ft.-long sections is nailed to the sidewall.

The point of my plumb bob was missing. As shown at right, a piece of threaded rod, filed to a point on one end and screwed into the plumb bob, made it as good as new.

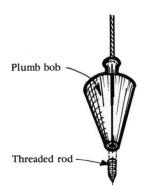

Plumb bob

Threaded rod

Apr. 27

Rain. Ordered skylights and saved $100 per skylight by shopping around. Ordered 1x12 rough cedar for trim and 20 squares of 18-in. red cedar roof shingles. Cut dormer-roof fillets on a bandsaw.

I cut a rafter fillet pattern for the dormer roofs using a radial saw. It worked, but cutting 18 1½-in.-thick rafter fillets on the bandsaw worked a lot better.

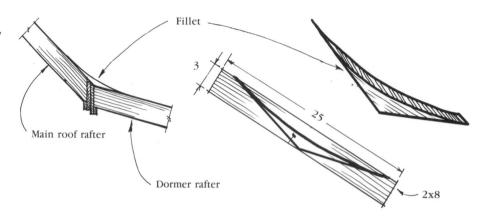

Fillet

Main roof rafter

Dormer rafter

3

25

2x8

Fillets (1½ in. thick) under the plywood on each rafter form the curve where the dormers meet the main roof. 8d common nails hold the plywood into the curve. The horizontal 2x4s nailed to the roof make climbing on the roof easier.

The rafter fillet at the edge of the dormer roof.

I thought I would have trouble, even with 8d common nails, pulling the plywood to the rafters at the fillets. But as shown here from the underside of the roof sheathing, the system worked well.

Apr. 28

Rain.

Apr. 29

Staged and sheathed north roof. My man with tendonitis showed up, so I put him to work studding the gable ends. It was too much for him, and he left early. The red cedar arrived: 20 squares is quite a load.

Apr. 30

Staged and prepared the south roof for sheathing. Blocking for upper skylight and sunholes.

Each sunhole has rafter tails extending through it. Every time there is an opening in sidewall or roof sheathing, the perimeter of the hole must have blocking to support the sheathing. There was a good bit of blocking here.

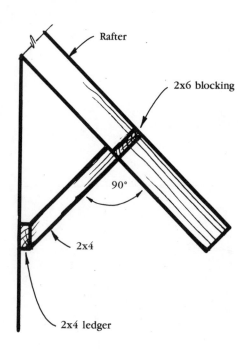

Rafter

2x6 blocking

90°

2x4

2x4 ledger

May 3

Finished all gable studding and sunhole blocking. Roof sheathing finished. Plumber still hasn't shown up. Town water hooked up.

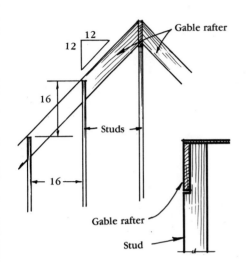

With a 12-in. in 12-in. pitch, each adjacent stud is 16 in. longer if the studs are spaced 16 in. on center.

May 4

Sheathed short north wall. Installed collar ties. Marked out second-floor interior partitions and cut all studs.

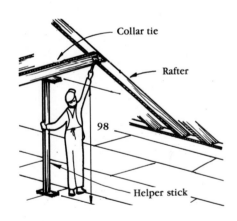

A helper stick is useful because it automatically sets the right height.

May 5

Ripped the 1x12 rough cedar for trim. Painted both sides of the cedar with Cabot's creosote stain, silver grey. Started the gable-end sheathing.

Wide pieces of scrap plywood, nailed to the faces of the studs, make a sturdy place to stack trim, as shown at right.

When ripping trim, as shown at far right, even pressure against the guide rail keeps cuts uniform.

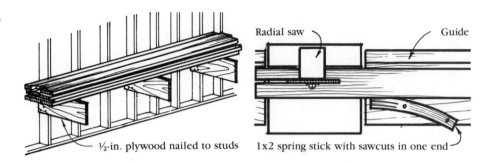

½-in. plywood nailed to studs   1x2 spring stick with sawcuts in one end

May 6

Finished sheathing dormer cheeks, gable ends and bits and pieces.

A 1x3 packing strip allows the siding to fit under the trim; 1x3 blocks on the roof locate the top of the rake board.

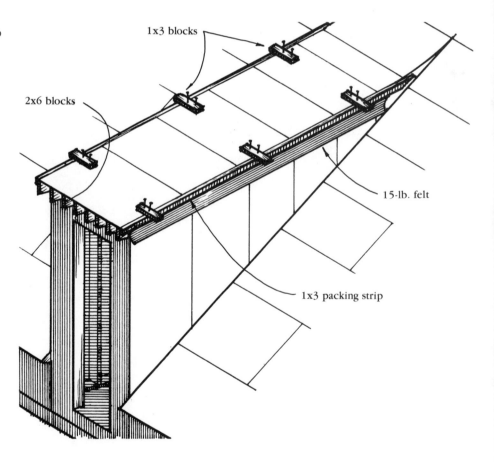

May 7

Started second-floor interior partitions. Installed 2x4 furring strips on the first-floor concrete walls in preparation for the Sheetrock.

May 10

Lower bedroom filled with sand, compacted and screeded in preparation for 6-mil polyethylene vapor barrier and 2-in.-thick foam floor insulation.

May 11

Finished trim except for around the sunholes. Started shingling the north side of the roof.

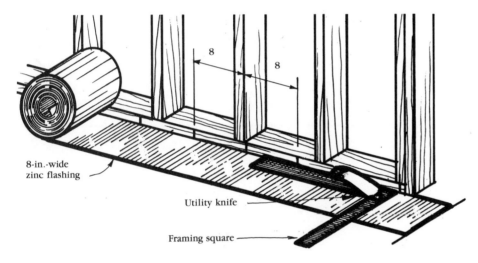

8-in.-wide zinc flashing

Utility knife

Framing square

When cutting many of the same size pieces of metal flashing, it's quicker to use a utility knife than tin snips. To speed up the job further, put a half-dozen or so marks spaced to the size required on the bottom plate of a partition. Use a framing square as a guide to make the cuts.

May 12

Roof shingling progressing. Cut hole for chimney. Trimmed out sunholes. I couldn't find my sharpening stone, so I improvised by using the flat face of a concrete pier.

I used ¾-in. roughsawn cedar to trim out the sunholes.

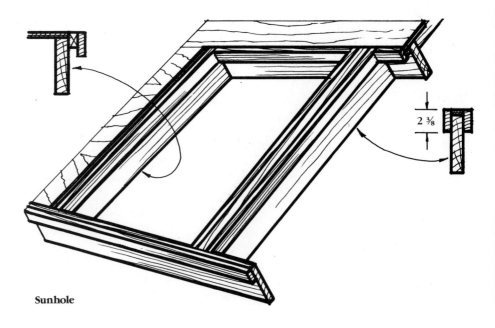

2 ⅜

Sunhole

May 13

Finished trim on dormers. Plumber showed up but just looked. Enlarged hole in concrete pilaster for heat trench. Started formwork for heat trenches.

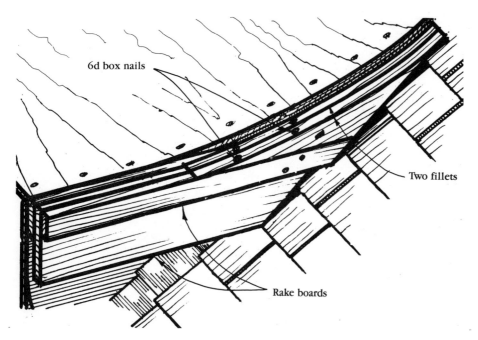

6d box nails

Two fillets

Rake boards

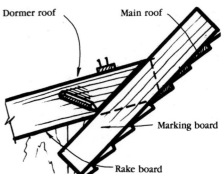

Dormer roof

Main roof

Marking board

Rake board

The straight pieces of the two-member rakes are nailed in place first. They are then followed by the rake-trim fillets, as shown at left. After gluing and nailing the rake-trim fillets in place, the final shaping is done.

To scribe the rake boards to the roof, I use a marking board to transfer the roof angle onto the ends of the rake boards, as shown above.

The rake trim has to follow the roof curve so rake-trim fillets were added to the straight rake members.

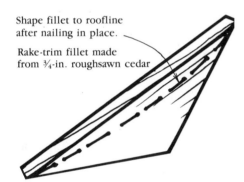

Shape fillet to roofline after nailing in place.

Rake-trim fillet made from ¾-in. roughsawn cedar

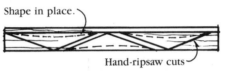

Shape in place.

Hand-ripsaw cuts

I had one small piece of the ¾-in. roughsawn cedar left with which to make the rake-trim fillets. I could have cut these simple triangles on the radial saw, but I chose to be safe and cut them with a hand ripsaw.

May 14

The plumber finally showed up and started. We worked together on the layout. Bedroom heat-trench formwork finished. Roof shingling continues.

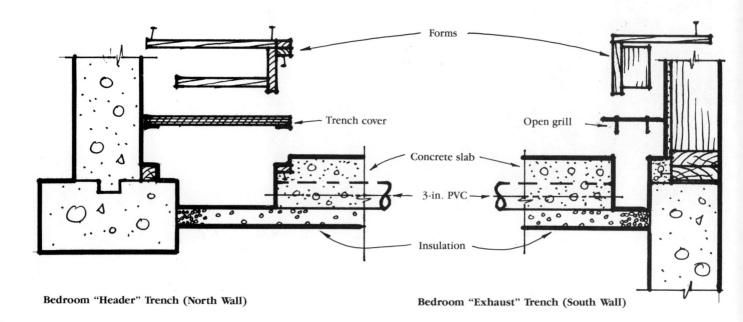

Bedroom "Header" Trench (North Wall)

Bedroom "Exhaust" Trench (South Wall)

To make the shingles more pliable, I considered soaking them in water, but 6d common galvanized nails, right, were all that were needed to hold the shingles to the curve of the roof.

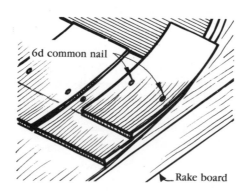

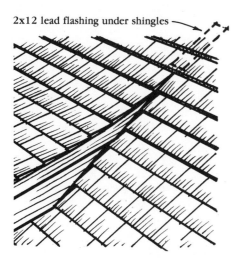

2x12 lead flashing under shingles

The dormer and main roof shingles have to meet sometime. It creates an odd condition, so I flashed the junction to make sure it wouldn't leak.

Three roof-section shingle courses—the dormer roof and the roof on each side of the dormer—must meet and be on the same plane. This requires a constant measurement check and sometimes a little fudging.

May 17

Worked out some roof-shingling problems.

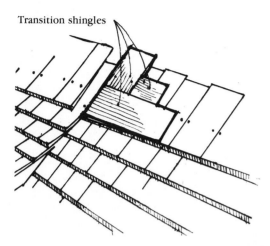

Transition shingles

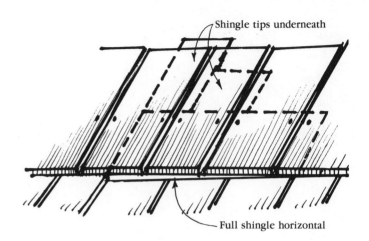

Shingle tips underneath

Full shingle horizontal

The shingle course on the dormer where it met the main roof was one shingle thickness above the main roof. Feathering the high course, as shown in the drawings above, brought it down without a noticeable bump.

The main roof trim and fascia are shown at right.

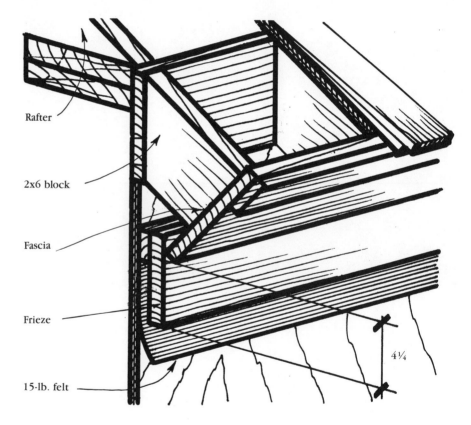

Rafter

2x6 block

Fascia

Frieze

15-lb. felt

4¼

May 18

Plumber finished drain work. Plumbing inspector gave his stamp of approval. Finished shingling the north roof. Started south roof. Heatbox skylight frame started.

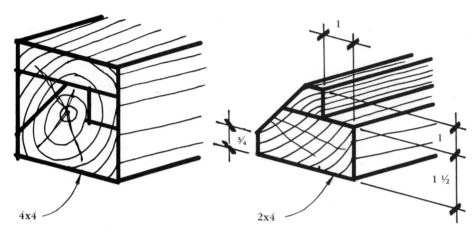

4x4

2x4

I started to cut the header for the heatbox skylight from a fir 4x4. After a very slow, smoky cut (about 2 ft. long), I gave up and worked out a way to make the header using 2x4s.

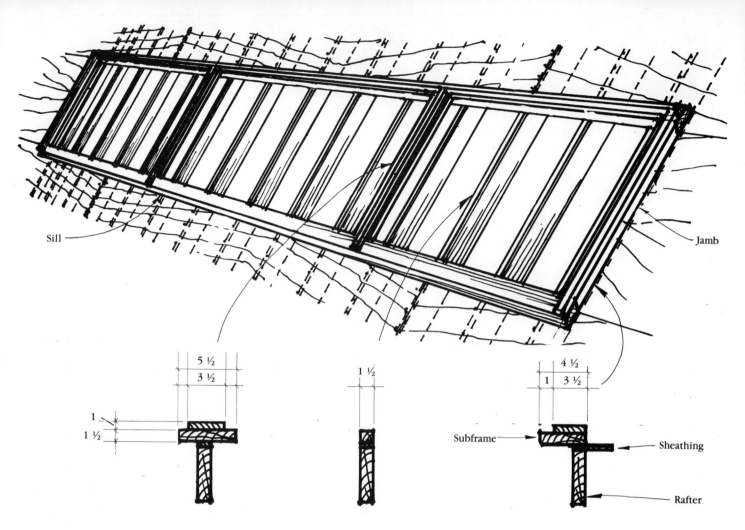

Sill

Jamb

5 ½

3 ½

1

1 ½

1 ½

4 ½

1   3 ½

Subframe

Sheathing

Rafter

There are four 1½-in.-wide intermediate rafters in each Plexiglas bay.

At right, the short starter shingles at the head of the sunholes bring the top shingles to the proper height. The exposed rafter tops and trim are shingled with 3½-in. wide shingles, which are cut on the tablesaw.

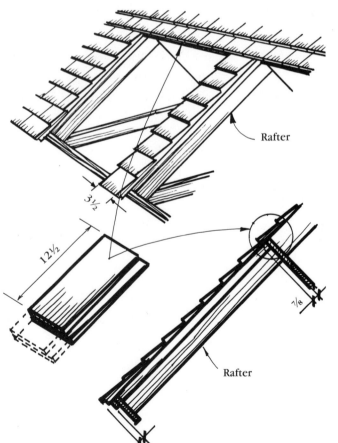

Rafter

3 ½

12 ½

7/8

Rafter

All the rough plumbing had to be done before the floor insulation and slab went in.

Here the sunholes, second-floor skylights and attic heatbox are ready for trimming.

Here the heatbox skylight is ready for flashing and glazing, but not until the next row of roof staging is set. It's a difficult job, even on good staging.

May 19

Removed staging from dormer fronts. Lower-level plumbing trenches backfilled, tamped and rough-graded. Started formwork for living room, kitchen and bath heat trenches. Shingling progresses.

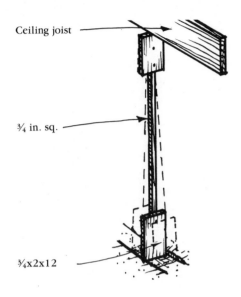

Ceiling joist

¾ in. sq.

¾x2x12

With this measuring stick, I sweep a 12-in. by 12-in. spot to screed to.

May 20

Roof shingling continues. Three skylights installed. Lower-level floor screeded to the proper level and then tamped before adding 6-mil polyethylene film and 2-in.-thick foam floor insulation.

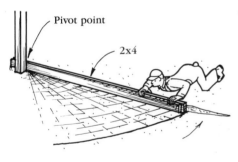

Pivot point

2x4

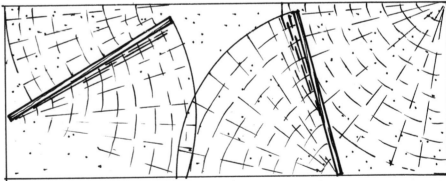

One person can do this work by bracing an end of the screed against a pivot point. The screed will roll over stones, large as well as small, so remove them. I criss-cross the screeding over the entire floor. The end result is a sand floor that is nice and flat, which will allow the insulation boards to lie flat.

May 21

Only one man showed up and not until noon. He continued shingling the roof. Formwork for heat trenches was finished, 3-in.-diameter PVC pipes laid in.

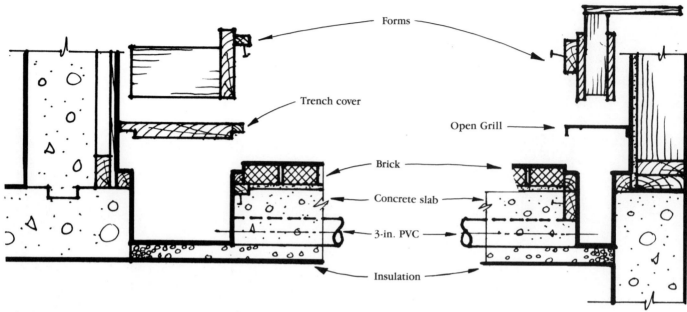

Living Room "Header" Trench (North Wall)

Living Room "Exhaust" Trench (South Wall)

The kitchen, bath and bedroom concrete slab is 2¾ in. higher than the living-room slab. The living room will get a brick floor and the kitchen, bath and bedroom will get 2x4 sleepers, plywood and vinyl, which will bring all the floors to the same level.

The measuring stick at right locates the top of the floor-slab form.

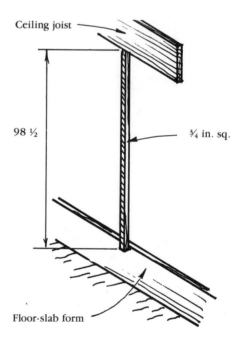

Laying In the Pipes

Drive against trench form.

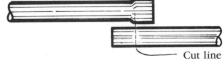

Cut line

2x4 block prevents damage to pipe.

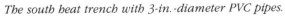

Drive this pipe against form

Stand on this pipe

When installing the pipes, first cut them to length, fit them between the forms, then snug them up against the form. Standing on one pipe holds it in place against one form while you are driving the other pipe over to the other form. The 2x4 block prevents damage to the pipe you're hammering.

The south heat trench with 3-in.-diameter PVC pipes.

The south heat trench with open floor grill.

May 24

Rain.

May 25

Two guys didn't show up. The roof continues. Concrete slab man showed up, he'll pour tomorrow. Cut the remainder of the trim (door casings, corner boards, etc.), and they're ready for staining. Cut and shaped the two 6x6 fir exterior corner posts for the cantilevered roof at the southeast and southwest corners.

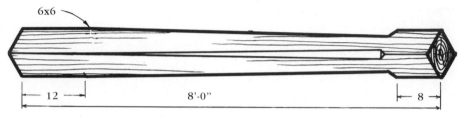

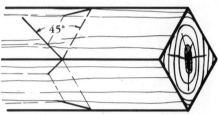

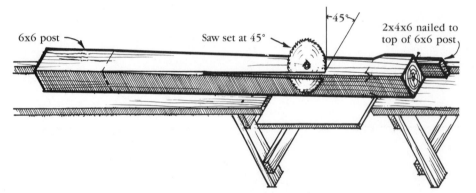

To cut the exterior corner posts, set the saw for ripping at a 45º angle. The saw starts 12 in. from the bottom and stops 8 in. from the top.

Finish the long angled cut with a hand ripsaw. Then cut the short 45º angle with a crosscut saw.

May 26

The roof continues. Concrete slabs were poured and the PVC pipes floated. Spent a frantic 30 minutes installing 2x4 braces to hold them down. No harm done, even though the 2x4s are still in the concrete. I set up the bedroom slab the right way while the living-room slab was being worked. The 2x4s were removed after the slab had been poured and the concrete had stiffened a little. We learn.

After the living-room pipes floated, I devised this 2x4 bracing system, which was removed after the concrete had set up a little. It worked slick.

A 12-in.-diameter flex-duct will run from the attic heatbox to the short section of trench below the window on the right, which connects with the north heat trench.

May 27

We really suffered from the sun on the south side of the roof today. Pulled the 2x4 braces from the concrete slab and patched the holes. Floor and chimney bricks delivered. Covered the bedroom slab with polyethylene film and 2x4s to slow down the curing, which makes for a harder surface. Picked up three roughsawn cedar 1x12x18' boards for the ridge cap. Ripped them to 5⅞ in. wide and the remaining pieces are 5 in. wide—perfect for each side of the ridge cap. Painted both sides with Cabot's creosote stain. Picked up ¼-in.-thick Plexiglas for the heatbox skylight. The skylight openings were framed for 38⅜x76⅜ Plexiglas. My Plexiglas measures 48x75, so I changed the framing.

May 28

Trimmed the overhanging roof shingles at the ridge. Finished the corner boards. Set staging for sidewall shingling. Big cleanup and a run to the dump.

The shingles on the north side are cut to a snapped chalkline at the ridge with a portable power saw. The south shingles are cut the same way.

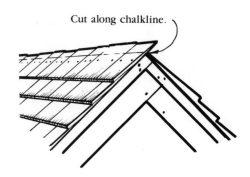

Cut along chalkline.

May 31

The roof shingling is done. Ridge boards are installed. All windows but one are installed, and that one is back-ordered.

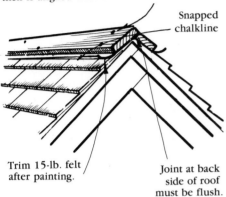

Wide ridge board nails at top to narrow board, then is aligned with chalkline and nailed.

Snapped chalkline

Trim 15-lb. felt after painting.

Joint at back side of roof must be flush.

The narrow (5-in.) ridge board is installed to a snapped chalkline on 18-in.-wide building paper stapled over the ridge shingles. The wide (5⅞-in.) ridge board is nailed at the top to the narrow ridge board. The bottom is aligned to a snapped chalkline and then nailed. The two boards must be flush at the joint.

Windows next to corners should be parallel to the corner boards. Windows close together should be parallel to each other. This looks good and makes for easier siding. Vinyl windows can have bowed rails, so take care when installing them.

First, locate the high side of the sill and drive the first nail, as shown in the drawing at right.

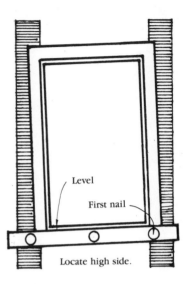

Level

First nail

Locate high side.

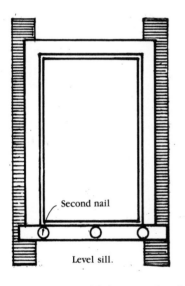

Second nail

Level sill.

Level the sill, then add the second nail.

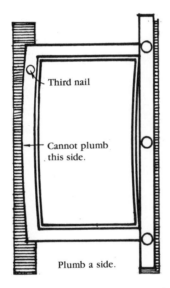

Third nail

Cannot plumb this side.

Plumb a side.

Plumb a straight side, then put in the third nail.

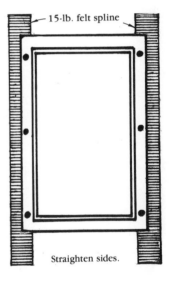

15-lb. felt spline

Straighten sides.

Straighten the sides and complete the nailing. The felt spline is part of the flashing system.

June 1

Started shingling the gable ends. Set two Plexiglas panels in the heatbox skylight. Pulled the forms from the concrete slab. The north form came easily, but the south form was stuck solid. It was one of those impossible jobs that somehow gets done. One man walked off the job because he was upset with his friend, a fellow worker. My son Richard came home from school and started work. His friend Charlie, the owner's son, came by, so I put him to work, too.

The packing strip under the rake board was too thin to allow the gable shingles to fit behind. The packing strip I have always used was a strong ¾-in.-thick one. It's now a weak ¾-in.-thick one.

I cut the face of the shingle following the rake board with a utility knife and finished the job with a sharp chisel.

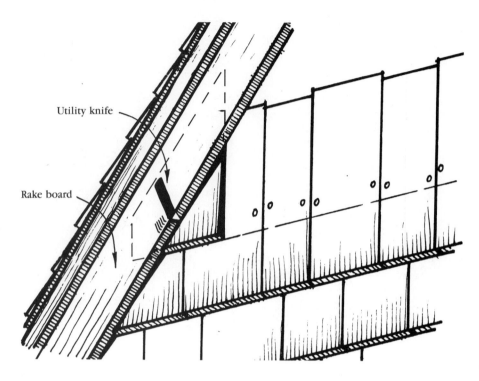

Utility knife

Rake board

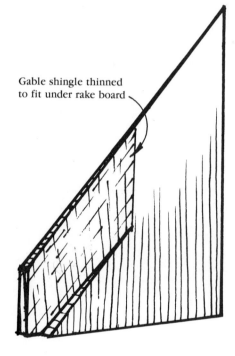

Gable shingle thinned to fit under rake board

June 2

The sidewall shingling continues. One window is still back-ordered, disrupting the shingling rhythm. Had a rainstorm that started a stream toward the basement window. I diverted the water through some 3-in.-diameter PVC pipe so that it ran along the front and side of the house. The next day we had a Grand Canyon where the pipe had been. The road-water runoff wants to make its path through the middle of the house—this will be a problem later. Started the formwork for the reinforced-concrete slab in the garage.

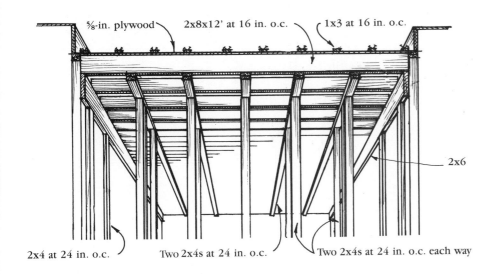

⅝-in. plywood   2x8x12' at 16 in. o.c.   1x3 at 16 in. o.c.

2x6

2x4 at 24 in. o.c.   Two 2x4s at 24 in. o.c.   Two 2x4s at 24 in. o.c. each way

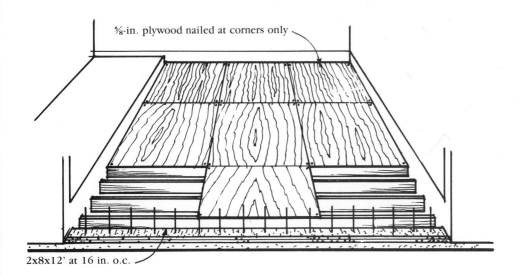

⅝-in. plywood nailed at corners only

2x8x12' at 16 in. o.c.

June 3

Sidewall shingling continues. Installed support posts (2x4x83) under the garage formwork. Built garage apron form. Cleaned the last pieces of Plexiglas. Had to scrape the paper off with a flat stick. It took two men two hours.

Posts are cut a tad short to allow for shingle-tip shims at the top. The shingle tips should be snug but not so snug that the joist above is raised, causing the adjacent post to be loose. All posts should be snug and then toenailed at the top and bottom.

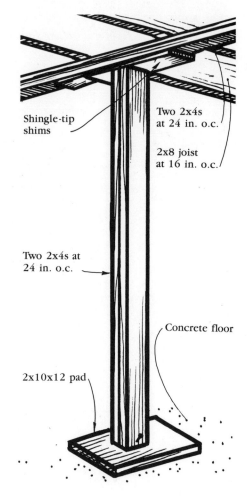

Shingle-tip shims

Two 2x4s at 24 in. o.c.

2x8 joist at 16 in. o.c.

Two 2x4s at 24 in. o.c.

Concrete floor

2x10x12 pad

June 4

One gable end shingled. Dormer cheeks started. Finished flashing the heatbox skylight.

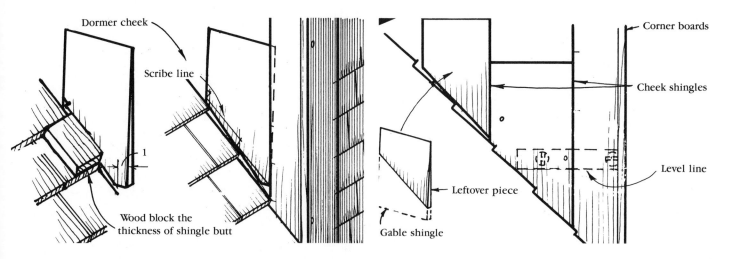

Dormer cheek

Scribe line

1

Wood block the thickness of shingle butt

Corner boards

Cheek shingles

Level line

Leftover piece

Gable shingle

I like to fit the shingles to the roof by scribing, as shown above.

I use the tip from a gable shingle to fill in next to the scribed shingle, as shown at above right.

Each course after the starter course at the bottom is started with a square shingle and the adjacent angled shingle scribed to the roof, as shown in the drawing at below left.

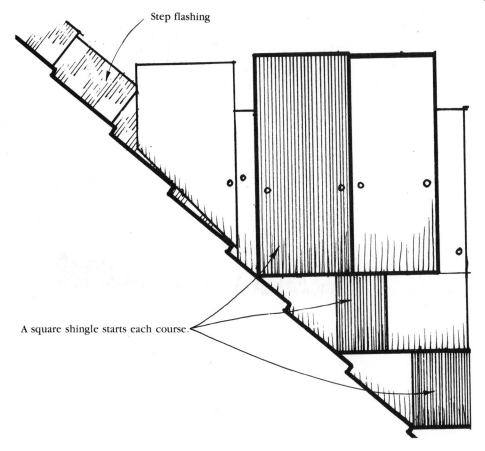

Step flashing

A square shingle starts each course.

The zinc step flashing at each shingle course is installed as the shingling progresses up the side of the skylights. The sill piece is the first to receive the lead flashing, followed by the jamb pieces. (I prefer aluminum flashing to lead flashing on long expanses, as the lead tends to break down, but aluminum flashing was unavailable at the time.) The head piece is then installed and the shingling continues over this piece. The jamb lead laps over the sill at the bottom and the step flashing at the sides. The head lead laps over the jambs. The sill lead runs under the glazing and folds over the 2x4 sill piece and is nailed. After the glazing is installed, the head and jamb lead folds over the wood stops and onto the glazing. To prevent long pieces of flashing from buckling due to expansion, it's best to use short sections lapped with slotted screwholes.

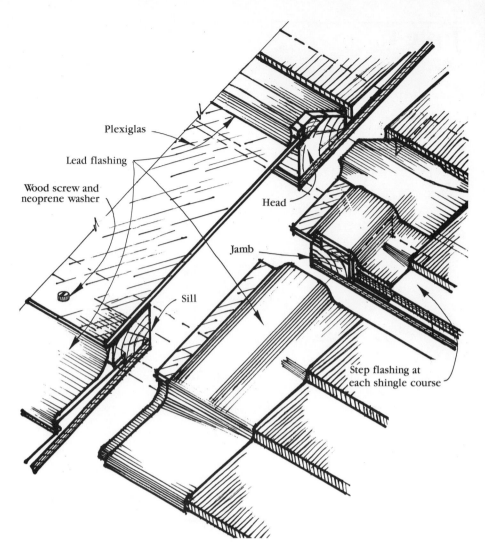

Plexiglas

Lead flashing

Wood screw and neoprene washer

Head

Jamb

Sill

Step flashing at each shingle course

June 5

Started the steel work for the reinforced-concrete slab in the garage. Shingling continues.

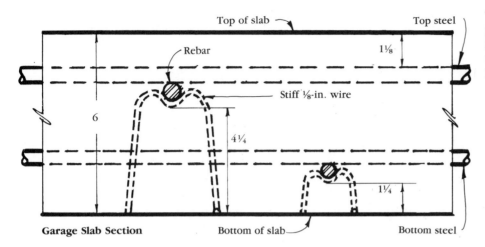

Garage Slab Section

The wire high chairs shown at left support the steel at the proper distance from the bottom of the slab. The bottom steel is 1¼ in. high; the top steel has a 1⅛-in. covering of concrete.

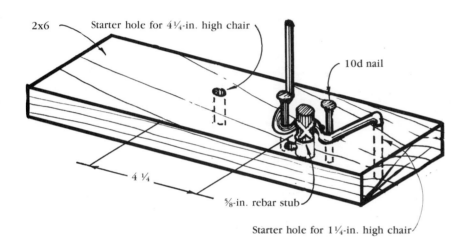

The placement of the 10d nails shown on this high-chair bending jig makes the short high chair. Repositioning one nail and starting the first bend 4¼ in. from the rebar stub makes the tall high chair.

June 7

Richard and I set the steel for the garage slab. It's best to have a structural engineer calculate the steel required for this type of concrete slab. The shingling continues.

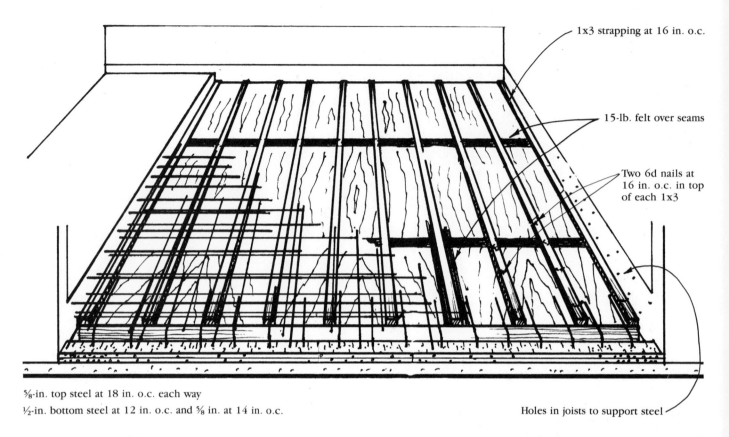

1x3 strapping at 16 in. o.c.

15-lb. felt over seams

Two 6d nails at 16 in. o.c. in top of each 1x3

⅝-in. top steel at 18 in. o.c. each way
½-in. bottom steel at 12 in. o.c. and ⅝ in. at 14 in. o.c.

Holes in joists to support steel

Shown above, 1x3 strapping at 16 in. on center is retained in the slab and is the nailing for the ceiling below.

The jig shown in the drawing at below left is good for cutting steel.

The scribing blocks shown in the drawing at below right locate steel-support holes in the side joists.

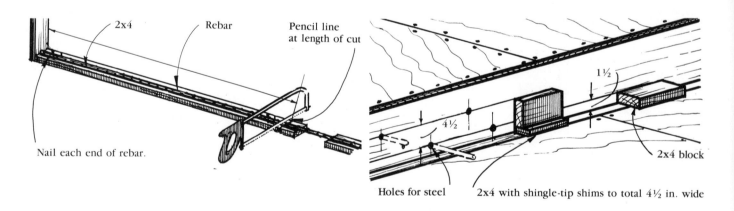

2x4

Rebar

Pencil line at length of cut

Nail each end of rebar.

1½

4½

Holes for steel

2x4 block

2x4 with shingle-tip shims to total 4½ in. wide

June 8

Finished the steel work. The shingling continues.

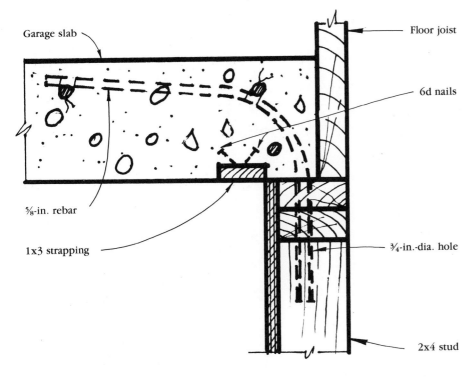

Garage slab

Floor joist

6d nails

⅝-in. rebar

1x3 strapping

¾-in.-dia. hole

2x4 stud

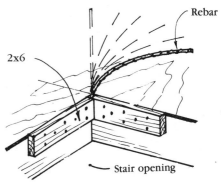

Rebar

2x6

Stair opening

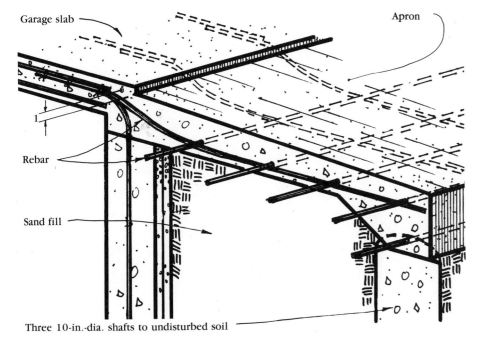

Garage slab

Apron

1

Rebar

Sand fill

Three 10-in.-dia. shafts to undisturbed soil

Five bent pieces of ⅝-in. rebar on each side of the garage slab tie to the upper steel in the slab and anchor in the partition below, as shown at left.

I used the jig shown above to bend the rebar. You put one end into the hole in the corner and then lean on the upper end—⅝-in. rebar is tough to bend, so I had to stand on it and kind of jump a little. I made sure I had a good handhold on something, in case the bar slipped.

The apron steel has an S-bend to allow for the 1-in. lip at the door opening. To support the outer edge of the apron, because it is on fill, I dug three 10-in.-diameter shafts down to undisturbed ground and filled them with concrete. A post-hole digger was the right tool for this job.

June 9

The shingling continues. Second-floor interior partitions plumbed and secured in place. The mason started the chimney. The concrete-slab man showed up unexpectedly and ready to pour. Had to get the door-sill form in place in a hurry. Made forms for the front steps and set them in place. My wife happened by and lucky for me—she got me a much needed post-hole digger. The tin knocker showed up to talk about the duct work. Stripped the staging from the roof after painting the ridge board and cutting off the 15-lb. building paper with a knife.

The apron should be an inch below the garage floor to keep water out. A quick way to form this is to nail a straight 2x4 on its face to the inside faces of the doorjambs. The edge of the 2x4 locates the beginning of the apron. The 2x4 should be a few inches wider than the door opening to allow for the track and the door to sit on the apron, which is lower than the garage-floor slab. The 2x4 should be level and supported at mid-span with a 1x3. (I've used a 1x4 instead of the 2x4, but it isn't as stiff and pushes out of shape easily.)

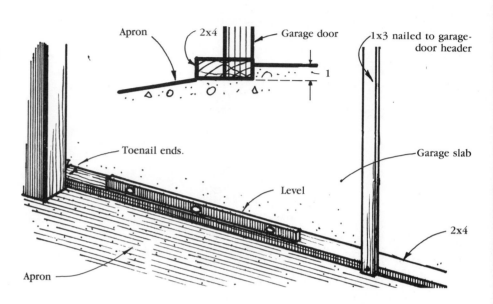

This supports the front-door landing.

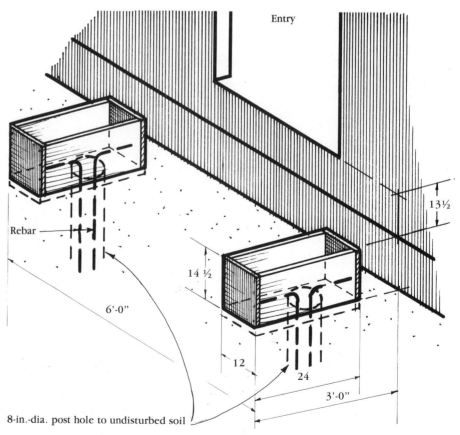

The reinforced-concrete garage slab is covered with polyethylene film to keep it wet. This will allow the concrete to achieve its maximum strength.

This is the forest that supports the garage slab. Polyethylene film is also on this floor. It has been almost three years and there are no cracks in either floor.

June 10

Racoons left their prints in the garage slab, a nice touch. The shingling continues. Went to the lumberyard to pick up the missing window, but it wasn't there. The truck left the yard without the window, so it must be at the other yard. I went there, but no luck. The driver had gone back for the window, and it was delivered to the job. I had wasted two trips and to top things off, it was the wrong window. After all that trouble and waiting, though, I decided the new window would work fine, and so I reframed for it. The mason started the brick floor in the living room. The radiant-heat man stopped by with his heat-loss figures and prices. Both were an improvement on the original estimates.

June 11

The dormer cheeks are finished, but I had to rip out a few courses because they looked so bad. The rest of the shingling continues. Trimmed the garage and front entry.

The shingler let the upper cheek courses get out of level. They had to be redone.

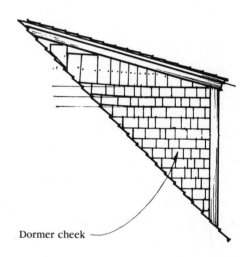

Dormer cheek

June 12

Stuccoed the exposed foam insulation on the foundation. The stucco is a must to protect the foam from damage from ultra-violet rays. Cement stucco on metal lath is the best system I know.

Here my mason, John Hilley, is doing the stucco work. I have done this work myself, and it is not too difficult.

The finished stucco with its 45° beveled edge blends in nicely with the 16-in. by 16-in. by 2-in. concrete patio blocks. The blocks are laid on compacted, leveled and screeded sand.

June 14

Rain.

June 15

All gables and dormer cheeks are finished. The front-wall shingling is started. Started the shiplapped soffit trim at the sunhole openings.

June 16

Shingling continues. The brick floor is finished except for cleaning it with acid.

June 17

The shingling is finished on the north side. Frieze boards in place on the entrance and garage. Finished the exterior doorjambs and casings. South, east and west lower-level shingling started.

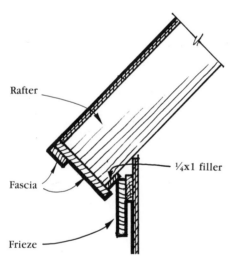

I wanted the fascia to meet the frieze, but it ended up about 1 in. away. A ¼-in. by 1-in. filler strip worked nicely.

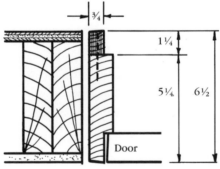

The exterior walls are 6½ in. thick, so a 1¼-in. by ¾-in. strip is glued and nailed to a stock doorjamb. It's a good setup for a screen door.

A ¾-in.-square stick nailed to the door frame keeps it parallel for installation. If the hinge side is nailed in place plumb, the other side will be plumb, too. The stick also aligns the jamb with the exterior sheathing.

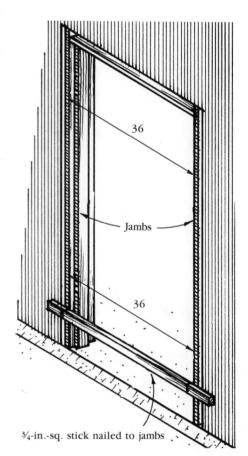

¾-in.-sq. stick nailed to jambs

June 18

The sidewall shingling continues.

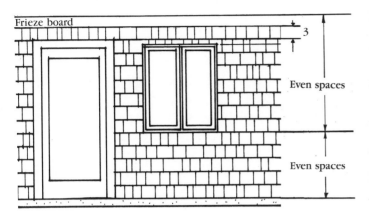

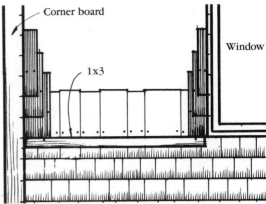

I had planned for the window and door headers to line up, but they didn't. It looked better to me with the shingle courses worked out as shown here.

Above the shingle course just finished, I like to set a shingle on three courses at each end. If it's a short run, I tack a straight 1x3 to the wall so that the upper edge is up against the butts of the lowest pair of shingles. The shingles for that course are then stacked along the 1x3 and nailed in place. A long course requires the extra step of snapping a chalkline between the shingles before nailing the 1x3 in place.

June 21

The sidewall shingling continues. A good carpenter can strip old shingles and put on new at the rate of one square a day. My men don't even come close. I let one man go today, not much more he can do on this job. Pulled the staging from under the garage slab, another success. Put wood sleepers on the bath and kitchen floors so that all the floors would be flush.

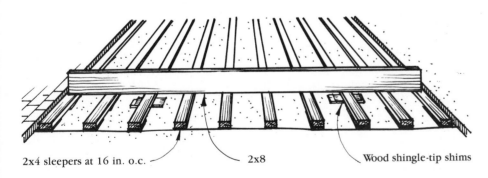

Shim and nail both sides, then shim the in-between sleepers to a straight 2x8.

2x4 sleepers at 16 in. o.c. —   2x8   Wood shingle-tip shims

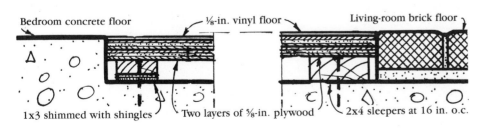

The variation in the slab made for different-thickness sleepers.

Bedroom concrete floor   ⅛-in. vinyl floor   Living-room brick floor

1x3 shimmed with shingles   Two layers of ⅝-in. plywood   2x4 sleepers at 16 in. o.c.

June 22

General cleanup outside. Finished sleepers and covered them with ⅝-in.-thick plywood from the garage forms.

When cutting wood that has been used in concrete, or painted, the blade is least affected when the teeth enter the cut on the clean side. With a portable power saw, the bad face is up. With a tablesaw, the bad face is down.

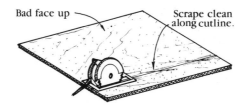

Bad face up

Scrape clean along cutline.

June 23

Started the lower-level interior partitions.

June 24

Strapped the ceiling with 1x3s at 16 in. on center.

Strapping is a means of straightening an uneven ceiling. The 1x3s are nailed to the underside of the ceiling joists, then shimmed out where necessary with the tips of wood shingles. Cape Cod is the only place I have seen this done. In fact, it used to be in the code.

June 25

Finished the attic heatbox.

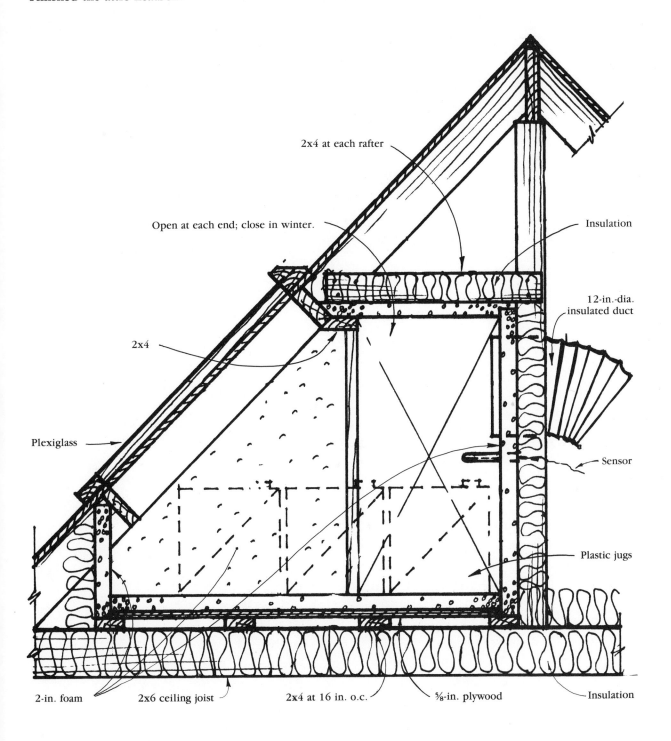

2x4 at each rafter

Open at each end; close in winter.

Insulation

12-in.-dia.
insulated duct

2x4

Plexiglass

Sensor

Plastic jugs

2-in. foam   2x6 ceiling joist   2x4 at 16 in. o.c.   ⅝-in. plywood   Insulation

The 21-ft.-long heatbox is the primary heat source of this house. A fan is connected to the 12-in.-diameter insulated flex-duct. The hot air is pushed under the lower-level floor to a continuous heat trench at the south edge of the floor. Thirty 6-gal. plastic jugs filled with water store the heat and a sensor controls the on/off switch.

The heatbox is made of 2-in.-thick foam walls and floor, covered on the outside with 3½-in. fiberglass insulation. Each end is opened for ventilation in the summer, then sealed for the winter. I haven't yet devised a simple system for opening and closing the ends. It has to be a hinged door that can be operated from the floor below by a sys-

tem of ropes and pulleys.

The 12-in.-diameter metal duct piece, shown on the right wall in the bottom photo on the following page, connects to the flex-duct that goes to the fan box on the floor below. The heat sensor is right next to this metal duct.

The attic space for the heatbox, with the skylight showing through the rafters.

The plastic water jugs in the heatbox had to be removed when one of them leaked the second year after completion of the house.

June 28

Exterior doors and hardware were delivered to the job. The electrician showed up. The tin knocker showed up and spent two hours figuring the ductwork for the heating system. Lower-level closets framed. Screwed horizontal 2x4 nailers to the north concrete wall. It was about 1 in. out of plumb, so 1x3 vertical strapping, at 16 in. on center, shimmed plumb, took care of that problem. It was easier to shim and nail vertical 1x3s to horizontal 2x4s than it would have been to shim the horizontal 2x4s screwed to the concrete wall.

June 29

Interior partitions almost finished. I am running out of 2x4s. I haven't ever ordered enough 2x4s when building a house. The electrician strung a few wires. The mason cleaned the brick with muriatic acid (four parts acid to one part water) and used plenty of water to rinse.

June 30

The plumber showed up late and left early. The electrician didn't show at all. Finished strapping the ceiling. Terrific rainstorm last night washed away a lot of the fill from around the house. Bulldozer didn't show, was due last week, yesterday and today. The big washout would have been avoided if the place had been graded. The building inspector informed me that he thinks a wood garage floor would have been okay as long as it was non-absorbing and could take a 75-pound-per-square-foot load. Now he tells me.

Jul. 1

The septic tank is in. The ductwork for the heat exchanger and attic heatbox is in. I used 6-in.-diameter insulated flex-duct for the heat exchanger and 12-in.-diameter insulated flex-duct for the heatbox. The plumber showed up to tell me he will be back Wednesday. That puts the Sheetrock schedule off two weeks. The electrician didn't show up again, so I had to put the insulation off a day. Started the wood blocking for the heat trenches.

The north heat trench will have a continuous solid-wood cover fastened to the blocking.

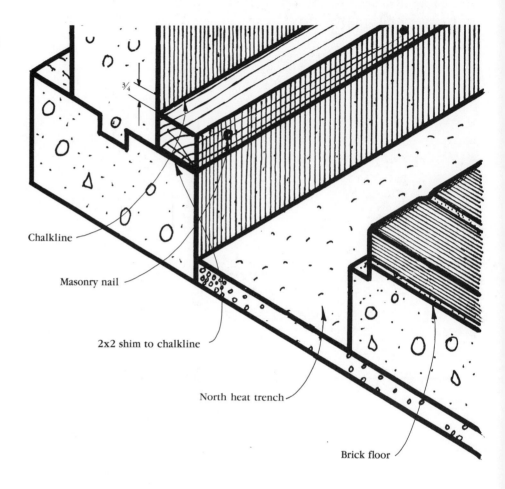

Chalkline

Masonry nail

2x2 shim to chalkline

North heat trench

Brick floor

It looks like they are laying someone to rest. It's a big hole, and I was a litle concerned that the house might follow the septic tank.

The overflow tank, at left, is almost as big as the septic tank.

The insulated flex-duct on the top right comes from the attic heatbox and connects to a fan in the metal box at the lower right. The flex-duct coming out of the metal box goes down to a trench that is connected to the north header trench.

The heat exchanger has one insulated 6-in.-dia. flex-duct for exhaust and one for intake. Both go to an exterior wall. The other two are for intake and exhaust within the house. Note the 2x4s scabbed to the bottoms of the rafters to allow space for insulation and air space above the insulation.

Jul. 2

Ready for insulation, but the insulation men didn't show up.

Jul. 6

Woke up with a bad cold, not much work today. A little backfilling going on. Insulation started.

Jul. 7

Insulation finished. Backfilling almost done. Picked up 70 bricks for the front steps and landing. Railroad ties for the retaining walls, window wells and front steps were delivered.

Jul. 8

Installed blocking for towel racks, shower rods and baseboards, to be ready for the Sheetrockers. Set up the plumber, electrician and subs for the driveway, backfilling and retaining walls, so they all know when to show up. But it doesn't always work out as planned.

Jul. 9

Too hot and humid, only half a day of work. Odds-and-ends things.

Jul. 10

Cleanup. Plumber and electrician showed up. Removed a few studs so shower and tub could get into the bathrooms.

Jul. 11

Checked and repaired the vapor barrier that was pulled off by the plumber and electrician. Final cleanup before the Sheetrockers begin.

The vapor barrier is installed on the warm side of the insulation to prevent moisture migration. As is usually the case, plumbers and electricians pull it aside when it's in their way. Rarely do they staple it back.

Jul. 12

Grading finished. Covered the brick floor to keep it clean. The Sheetrock was delivered. The plumber and electrician finished just before the rockers arrived on site. The road in front of the house was bermed by the town to direct road-water runoff to a catch basin down the hill. It almost worked.

Jul. 13

Telephone wires roughed in. Sheetrock work started.

Jul. 14

Sheetrock work continues.

Jul. 15

Sheetrock work continues.

Jul. 16

Sheetrock work continues. Had to lower the bathroom ceiling to cover the plumbing. Ordered 5 gal. of #7 clear Hydrozo water repellent to seal the brick floor.

Jul. 19

Sheetrock work continues. Both asphalt driveways started.

Jul. 20

Sheetrock work continues. Both asphalt drives finished. A 2-ft.-long piece of railroad tie was put in front of the driveway to keep cars off. We had a heavy rain that afternoon and the tie diverted the road water over the berm, down the driveway and into the window well. The water spilled into the house. It took a while to discover the problem was at the driveway and the tie, and there was a lot of frantic bailing at the window well. The spillway at the bottom of the driveway alongside the house started to erode. More frantic work filling the bottom of the spillway with rocks. Two more problems solved, but I was one wet, muddy carpenter.

Jul. 21

The Sheetrock is finished. Garage door with auto-opener is in. Three stair carriages cut and installed. Exterior doors planed to fit the openings. Moved the shiplapped red cedar soffit material and twenty-eight 2x8x12' planks from one end of the house to the other to make room for the meter box.

Jul. 22

Measured and ordered interior trim material.

Jul. 23

Repaired leaking skylight. Two men picked up the interior trim and plywood underlayment. Hung three exterior doors. Started to put the knobs on the doors, but the lock-bore kit I rented was the wrong one.

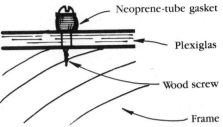

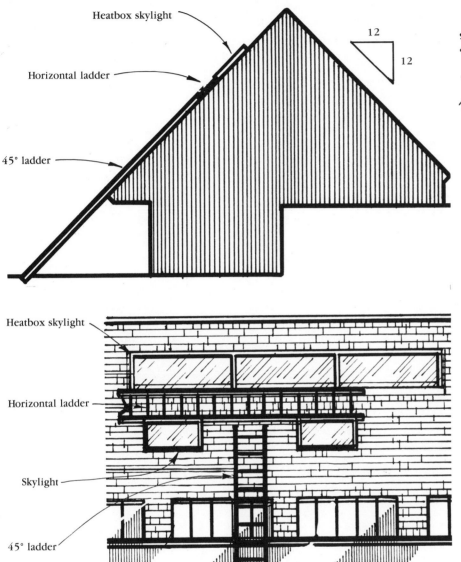

One Plexiglas sheet on the heatbox slipped, leaving an opening for rain. I had fastened the bottom of each sheet with two wood screws, but they worked loose and had to be replaced with longer screws. (Neoprene gaskets, sliced from tubing, seal the holes in the Plexiglas.)

A ladder along the roofline worked well for getting to the heatbox skylight. A horizontal ladder resting on the skylights below was adequate staging. The Plexiglas had to be removed and reset. A difficult job, but I used longer screws this time.

Jul. 24

The retaining-wall man didn't show up. I was to help him with the front landing and steps. Removed the plastic sheet from the brick floor and concrete floor. The brick floor has many white Sheetrock spots where the plastic was punctured. Scraping with a fingernail worked pretty well, but it was tough on the hands. Cleaned the Sheetrock chunks from the heat trenches. Hung and painted the front door. Installed underlayment. Rough-cut all window trim. Designed newel posts and railing. Picked up stair material, treads, risers and stringers. Brought in my tablesaw, electric miter box and a Rockwell Sawbuck. Cabinet man arrived with all the cabinets. Both bathroom cabinets installed and most of the kitchen cabinets.

The 4-in.-square newel post is a good size, but the 4-in.-tall section at the top would have looked better at 6 in. square. The ½-in. groove in the rail is to receive ½-in.-square steel rods.

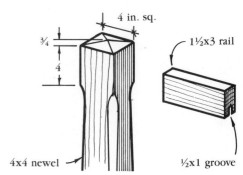

Jul. 27

Finished nailing off the underlayment just as the sheet-vinyl men arrived. One of the pieces of stair-stringer material was only 9 ft. long, and I needed it to be 10 ft. long. Another trip to the lumberyard. The electrician backed off the driveway onto a piece of 8x8 railroad tie, puncturing his gas tank. A full tank of gas drained onto the driveway toward the window well. A quickly dug trench diverted it to a quickly dug hole. Fortunately it was a rainy day and the only damage was a softening of the edge of the asphalt driveway. The cabinet work is finished.

Jul. 28

Rough-cut to length all interior window trim (extension jambs, sills, casings and aprons). Repaired another leaky skylight. My roofers put the head flashing under the step flashing at the sides of the skylight. Instead of water running over the step flashing, it ran under and into the house. I caught it before there was damage to the Sheetrock. The landscaper started with the plants and rocks.

Jul. 29

Cleanup on the upper level. Repositioned the flex-duct in the attic heatbox. The Sheetrockers pulled the duct off and it no longer reached the old hole. I had to plug the old hole and cut a new one. Put the flex-duct back on the heat exchanger. Betty, the owner, moved her belongings into the garage.

Jul. 30

Set the exterior 6x6 corner posts under the cantilevered roof at the southeast and southwest corners. Installed locksets in the lower-level doors.

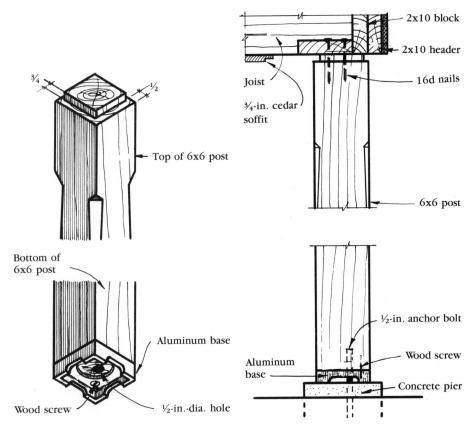

The post tops are cut back to receive the ¾-in. soffit, as shown at far left.

The bottoms of the posts are positioned on a ½-in. anchor bolt in a concrete pier, as shown at left.

Jul. 31

Set front-entrance lockset. Helped set the railroad ties at the front steps and landing. Window well finished.

I had wanted a gravel bottom for better drainage. I got sand instead.

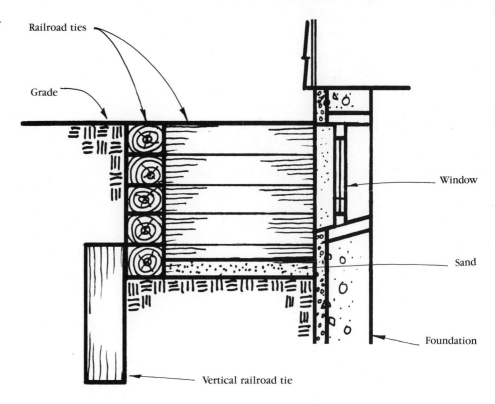

Railroad ties

Grade

Window

Sand

Foundation

Vertical railroad tie

Bricks will fill in between the railroad ties.

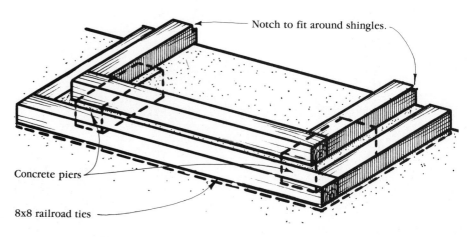

Notch to fit around shingles.

Concrete piers

8x8 railroad ties

Aug. 2

Set the interior stair posts. Cut the skirt boards, the trim pieces that run the length of the stairway on each side. Landscaping finished. Window trim continues.

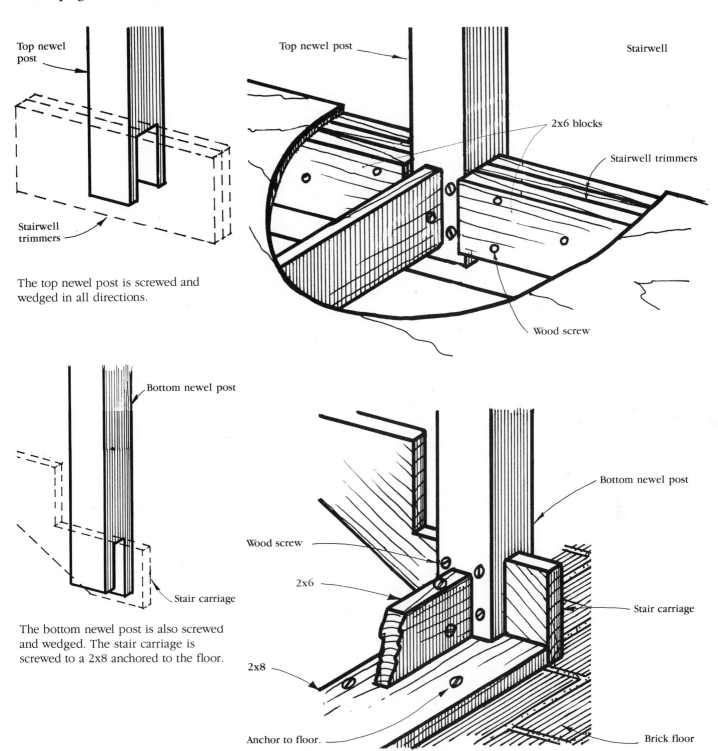

Top newel post

Stairwell trimmers

The top newel post is screwed and wedged in all directions.

Top newel post

Stairwell

2x6 blocks

Stairwell trimmers

Wood screw

Bottom newel post

Stair carriage

The bottom newel post is also screwed and wedged. The stair carriage is screwed to a 2x8 anchored to the floor.

Wood screw

2x6

2x8

Anchor to floor.

Bottom newel post

Stair carriage

Brick floor

I was concerned about making the newel post secure in the brick floor. There is not much to nail to. Fastening and bracing it to the stair carriage did the trick nicely.

Aug. 3

Rough-cut the remainder of the trim. Set stair stringers. Cut and fit risers. Ripped treads to width.

Aug. 4

Installed treads and risers. Door frames assembled and installed.

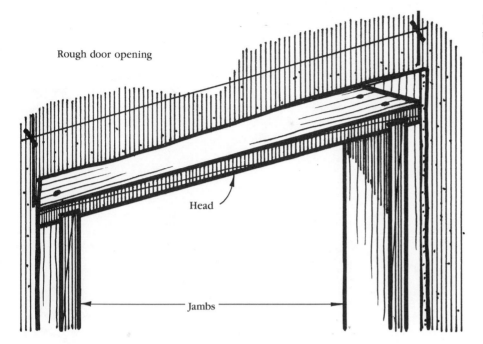

Rough door opening

Head

Jambs

I cut the head piece of the door frame to the width of the rough opening. Plumbing the jambs is then easy work.

Aug. 5

Plumbers installed sinks, toilets and shower and tub fixtures. Installed stair treads.

Aug. 6

Interior door frames finished. Relieved the backside of casings. Cut handrails. Cut and fit stair trim.

Aug. 7

Picked up 4¼-in.-wide oak nosing and oak scotia trim, which is used under the nosing, for stairs. Set brick in front step and landing.

Crowning the brickwork at the center allows water run-off, preventing future sagging in the middle.

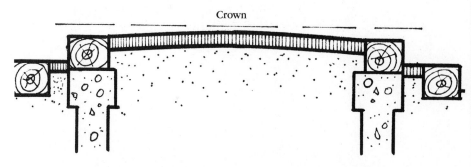

The sand should be well compacted before the bricks are installed.

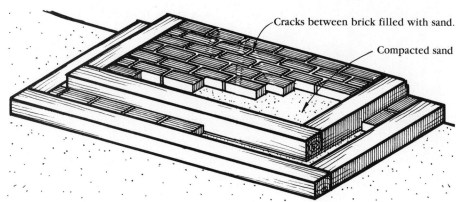

The slope allows water to run away from the house.

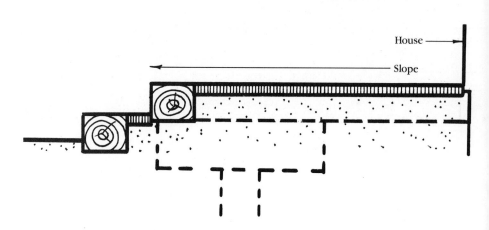

The brick and railroad-tie entry steps.

Aug. 9

Plumber almost finished. Telephones installed. Window trim continues. Cut and fit trim around stairwell and balcony. Relieved backside of head casings. Cut stair handrail to fit.

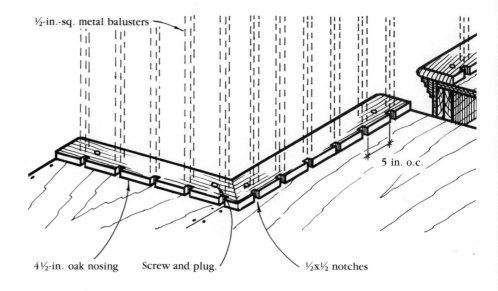

½-in.-sq. metal balusters

5 in. o.c.

4½-in. oak nosing Screw and plug. ½x½ notches

Aug. 10

Shaped handrails with a router. Finished stair trim. Window trim continues. Heavy rain ran over road berm, down driveway and into the window well. The town will make berm higher and the front yard will have to be graded to keep water away from the window well.

The ¾-in. by 4½-in. oak trim piece was shaped with a router. The Sheetrock runs up behind it.

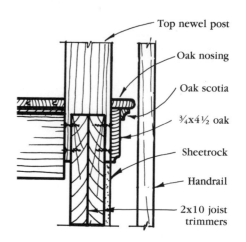

Top newel post

Oak nosing

Oak scotia

¾x4½ oak

Sheetrock

Handrail

2x10 joist trimmers

Aug. 11

Window trim continues. Picked up oak from the lumberyard. General cleanup on both levels. The floor people didn't show up.

Aug. 12

Window-trim man didn't show. Floor people started, need two more bundles of flooring. Began exterior soffit trim.

Aug. 13

Picked up three bundles of oak flooring (one extra to be sure). Floor-laying finished. Window trim almost finished on the lower level. Door trim started. Designed baseboard shape. Soffit work continues. Kitchen appliances arrived. The kitchen counter was made for a free-standing range, not the drop-in range that arrived. The range cannot be returned, so the counter will have to be modified. Topsoil spread and graded.

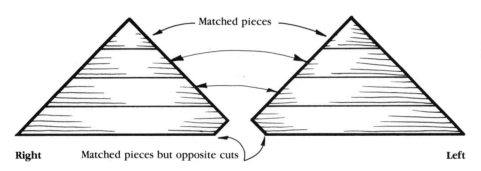

Matched pieces

Right   Matched pieces but opposite cuts   **Left**

I cut all the shiplapped pieces for the roof openings. They are matching pieces except for the bottom ones, which are opposites.

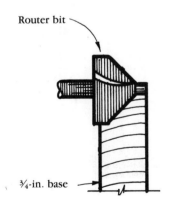

Router bit

¾-in. base

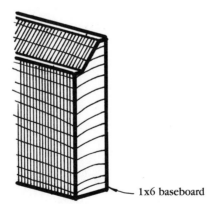

1x6 baseboard

The baseboard is cut with a router and chamfering bit.

Aug. 14

Finished the entrance landing. Redid the window well. Landscaper doing his thing.

I put a layer of building paper (15-lb. felt) on the outside face of the railroad ties and 2 ft. of gravel in the bottom of the window well. This will keep water away from the window.

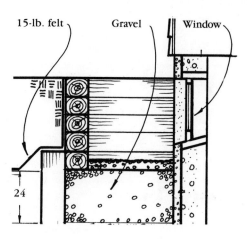

Aug. 16

Interior door trim continues. Exterior soffit finished. Oak floors and stairs sanded and sealed with first coat of polyurethane. Exterior trim work continues.

Two door casings meeting in a corner look better if the headers are the same height. The door framer didn't take this into account and the casings didn't match. The solution was to lower the casing on the sliding closet doors and cut the doors to match.

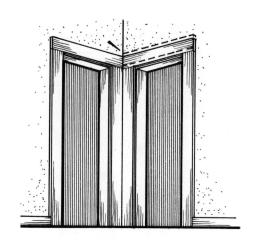

Aug. 17

The instant lawn was laid in. Exterior trim finished. Interior trim continues. Oak floor sanded and the second coat of polyurethane applied.

Aug. 18

Lots of company checking out this unusual house. Checked the oak flooring and it is the worst sanding job I have ever seen. It will have to be resanded. I usually do the flooring, but did not have the time this time. North heat-trench cover in the living room finished. Cut ½-in. by ½-in. steel balusters.

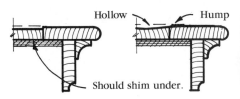

Hollow   Hump

Should shim under.

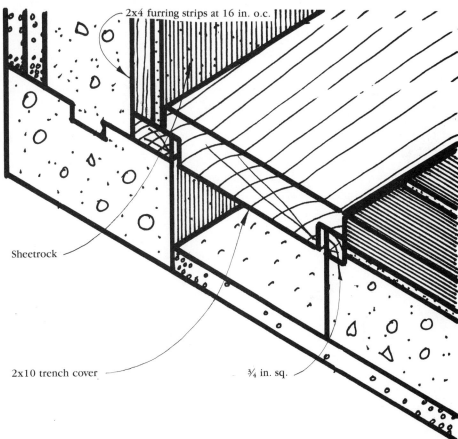

2x4 furring strips at 16 in. o.c.

Sheetrock

2x10 trench cover

¾ in. sq.

The nosing was a tad thicker than the oak flooring, so the floor man tipped the sander to cut off the edge of the nosing, above. The result was a depression all along the nosing. The nosing should have been sanded flat on top.

The north trench feeds the PVC pipe leading to the south exhaust trench. The north trench is covered, as shown at right; the south trench has an open grill. The north trench cover in the living room is in two pieces. One is a 100-in.-long 2x10 piece of spruce sealed in place with caulking and screws. The other is an 86-in.-long 2x10 piece of pine that is removable so that the trench may be cleaned.

Cutting ½-in. by ½-in. steel balusters was easy with a jig and a reciprocating saw with a metal-cutting blade.

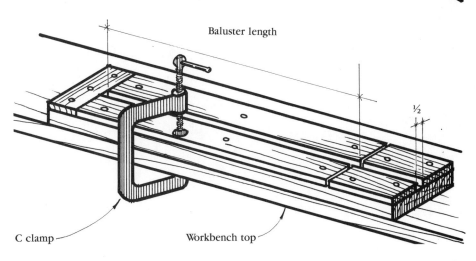

Baluster length

½

C clamp

Workbench top

Aug. 19

North trench cover in bedroom finished. South heat-trench blocking started.

The bedroom trench cover is also in two pieces. Both are made of plywood and are removable. A small section in the bathroom is also removable.

Aug. 20

Lower-level cleanup. Concrete bedroom floor given first coat of finish: one part Minwax Jacobean stain and two parts polyurethane, applied with a roller. Brick living-room floor given first coat of Hyrozo #7 clear, applied with a roller.

Aug. 21

Cleanup outside. Second coat put on bedroom and living-room floors. Painted steel balusters. Oak floor sanded again, it could be better.

This is a quick way to paint the balusters. The ½ in. of steel that sits on the 2x4s will be buried in the floor and rail.

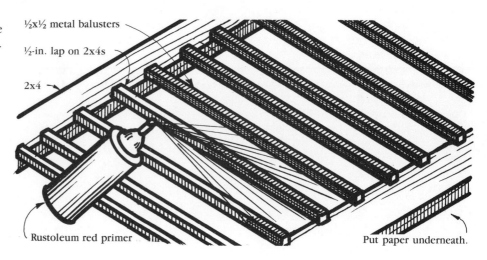

½x½ metal balusters

½-in. lap on 2x4s

2x4

Rustoleum red primer

Put paper underneath.

Aug. 22

Oak floor buffed and a third coat of polyurethane applied. Set stair handrail. Final coat on brick floor: one part turpentine and one part spar varnish, applied with a roller. Two quarts of varnish just made it. Going away for a week. Two men will carry on with the interior trim.

The upper-level rails at the stairs and balcony. The two grills in the ceiling are for the heatbox air intake and the heat exchanger.

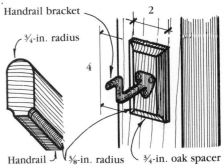

The rail bracket had to be packed out to allow the rail to clear the nosing comfortably. The 3/8-in. radius cut in the spacer matches the radius in the rails.

Aug. 27

Back from my trip—not much work has been done because of the potent fumes from the floor finish.

Aug. 28

Installed the steel balusters. Set rails in place.

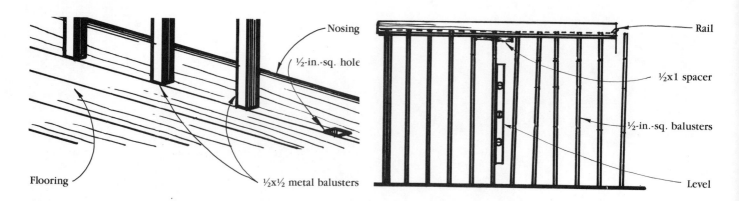

Nosing

½-in.-sq. hole

½x½ metal balusters

Flooring

Rail

½x1 spacer

½-in.-sq. balusters

Level

Half-inch holes squared with a chisel made for a tight fit, as shown in the drawing at above left.

Each ½-in. by 1-in. spacer was custom-cut to make each baluster plumb, as shown at above right.

The rail is screwed to the wall and at all mitered joints, right.

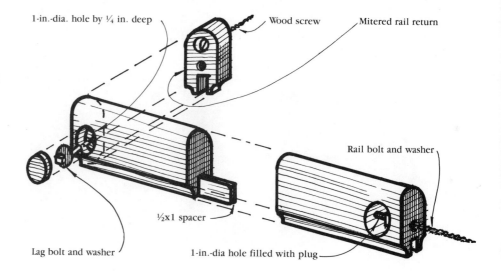

1-in.-dia. hole by ¼ in. deep

Wood screw

Mitered rail return

Rail bolt and washer

½x1 spacer

Lag bolt and washer

1-in.-dia hole filled with plug

Aug. 30

Railing work. Hired another man to help with the interior trim. Baseboards started. Last interior door hung. Bored holes for interior-door locksets. Closet shelves started.

Aug. 31

Closet-shelf work continues. Baseboard work continues. Metal grill for the south heat trench picked up at the welder's shop. Furniture comes tomorrow; it's another month's rent if it stays at the warehouse. The furniture will be set in the middle of each room, which will make it difficult to work. This move required a major cleanup.

The bedroom grill is in two pieces. To make it fit, ¼ in. had to be trimmed off one end.

The living room/kitchen grill is in five pieces and fits perfectly.

Sept. 1

Furniture was to arrive at 10:00 a.m., but it arrived at 12:00 noon. My new man, Doug, arrived and did a whale of a job. He set most of the baseboard on the lower level. The closet-shelf work continues. The worst rainstorm of the year dropped 4 in. of rain that night. The front yard was a small pond.

A catch basin and discharge line will have to be installed. The town catch basin down the road washed out for the third time.

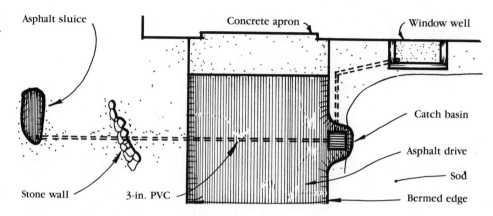

Sept. 3

Picked up more baseboard material at the lumberyard, then shaped it. Doug installed most of the baseboard on the upper level after casing four doors. Spray-painted the south heat trench with Rustoleum red primer.

Sept. 4

Installed baseboard in three lower-level closets. Set 7/16-in. by 2-in. doorstops on lower-level door frames. Betty and friends filled nailholes and painted Knot Stop over knots. I am leaving for a week and Doug is doing his own work, so that leaves one man to carry on.

Sept. 15

Work done while I was away: catch basin started, interior painting, front entry and utility-room shelves finished, all doorstops cut and fitted, landscaper started patio blocks, window trim finished. I am back on the job. Poured catch-basin and window-well slabs. Set the top section of 18-in. flue tile for the catch basin. Backfilled everything.

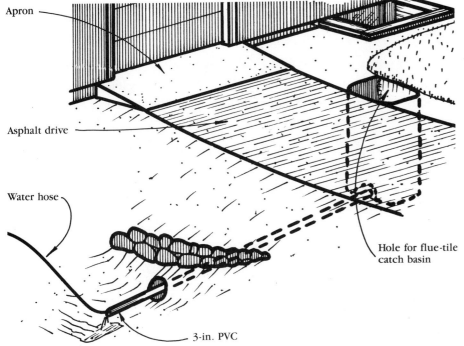

Apron

Asphalt drive

Water hose

3-in. PVC

Hole for flue-tile catch basin

That one window caused a lot of problems. I misjudged the amount of rainwater the road in front of the house directed onto the lot. The road is a gentle hill and the lot is halfway up the hill—the problem would be at the bottom of the hill, at the catch basin. I was right about the bottom of the hill, as the catch basin washed out three times, but the front yard received more than its share of water.

It took three tries, using a water hose inside a piece of 3-in.-diameter PVC, to get the pipe connected to the bottom of the 18-in. flue-tile catch basin.

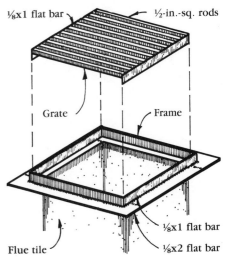

¾-in.-deep cut

Hand maul

18x18 flue tile

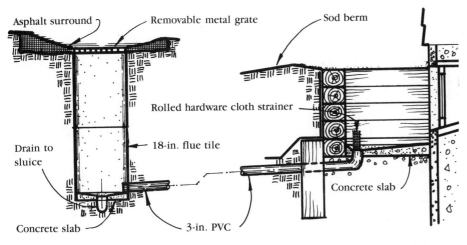

Asphalt surround

Removable metal grate

Sod berm

Rolled hardware cloth strainer

18-in. flue tile

Drain to sluice

Concrete slab

3-in. PVC

Concrete slab

The concrete slabs in the window well and catch basin are pitched to a plastic elbow drain, as shown above.

Cutting halfway through the walls of the flue tile with a masonry-cutting disk made it easy to break 2½ in. off the top. A hand maul, shown at above right, worked well for that.

The catch-basin cover/frame, at right, was made at a welding shop. It's set with an asphalt surround.

⅛x1 flat bar

½-in.-sq. rods

Grate

Frame

Flue tile

⅛x1 flat bar

⅛x2 flat bar

Sept. 16

Finished odds and ends of baseboard. All doorstops nailed. Attic access in garage ceiling trimmed and a hatch fitted. Framing for a new entry closet started. Checked the house for things to complete.

Sept. 17

Patio-block man quit, he didn't get much done. I will have to finish the job. New entry-closet work continues. Installed 4-in. by 8-in. metal grills in heatbox vents in upper-level ceiling. Installed a cat door in garage door. Put mid-shelf closet-pole support in the lower-level closet. Trimmed bottom of bathroom door. Raised the upper pole and lowered the lower pole in lower-level closet to fit blouses and skirts.

Sept. 18

Installed lower-level bathroom shelf. Installed towel and toilet-paper racks. Taped and spackled a small section of wall under the living-room stairs. Taped and spackled the entry closet. The closet doors in the entry were framed wrong so a few inches had to be cut off the bottom of the doors.

It should have been framed as shown at right. Instead it was framed as shown at far right....

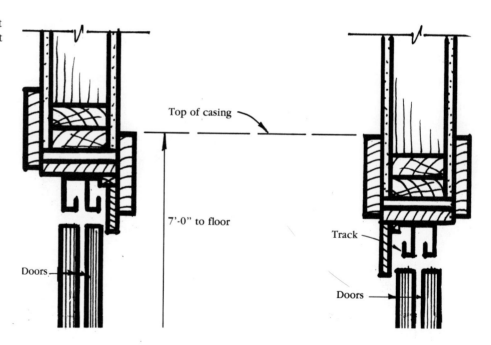

Sept. 20

Front entry finished. Skylight screens installed. Interior painting continues. Installed odd pieces of baseboard. Custom-built bookcases installed in living room. Spackling here and there. The catch basin works well.

Oct. 24

Electrician set heatbox controls for 80° on and 75° off. Split-rail fence installed at the bottom of the driveway. One layer of railroad ties set along the south patio.

Oct. 25

Moved and leveled four yards of sand for the patio-block bed. Set concrete patio blocks.

Oct. 26

Filled thirty 6-gal. plastic jugs with water and installed them in the heatbox.

Oct. 27

Checked the operation of the heatbox. It goes on at 9:00 a.m. and runs until 4:00 p.m. (daylight saving time). Patio work continues.

Nov. 2

Finished the patio blocks. Reset the heatbox controls to go on at 90°. The upstairs temperature is 80°.

Nov. 3

Installed a small wood gutter over the front-entry door.

The gutter is 7 ft. long and is open at both ends.

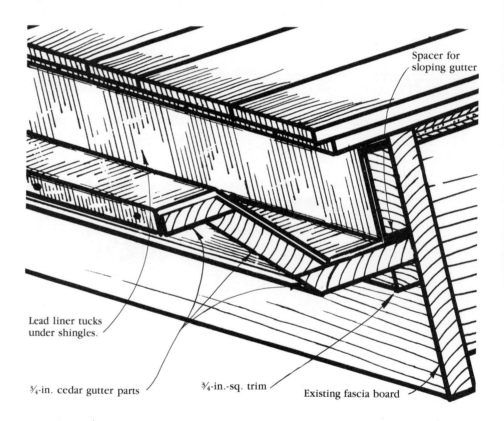

Spacer for sloping gutter

Lead liner tucks under shingles.

¾-in. cedar gutter parts

¾-in.-sq. trim

Existing fascia board

The north side of the completed house.

The south side of the house.

Epilogue

A house is rarely finished when it is "finished." There are always things that have to be done, and in the case of an innovative and experimental house, checking performance is part of the job.

The first call-back I got was for another leaky skylight. It was the same problem I had earlier—a loose screw in the corner of the Plexiglas. I had already put in longer screws with the first repair job, but I remembered one screw that didn't grab. I had a feeling it should have been replaced with a longer screw, but it was a hot day and I would have had to climb down the ladder and search for the right-size screw. The thirty minutes saved that day cost me three hours six months later.

The first really cold spell of the first winter started to freeze the hot-water pipe to the bathroom sink on the upper level. I managed to avoid a solid freeze by running the hot water. There was no further problem that winter. There should have been no problem at all, because the plumber covered the pipes with foam sleeves and there was fiber-glass insulation all around these pipes.

That winter also showed up a mistake the concrete man made when pouring the garage floor. I had asked that the slab be positively sloped out toward the garage door. I did not want any water sitting on the slab. The left rear corner of the slab is high, but the right rear corner is low, and all the melted ice and snow from the car runs right for that corner. The kitchen below is where the water seeped down to. Caulking the garage floor at the back and sides prevented further leaks. The floor could be built up with an epoxy product, but that would be very costly.

The first winter showed that the solar-heating system worked great. A wood stove was also to be used for heat and there were radiant-heating panels in the ceiling for back up. The radiant heat would not be used much, so I did not pay much attention to its requirements—I let the installers take care of that. Betty decided against using the wood stove for a variety of reasons, which made the radiant-heating system more important. I had not used this system before and did not realize it required insulation above it. The upper level is good, with the ceiling joist bays filled with 12 in. of fiberglass. The lower level had no insulation between the floors, which allowed the heat to radiate up as well as down. It makes sense and I think the installers should have said something. We ended up with a very warm second floor and a warm garage slab. The lower level only got half its heat. Fortunately, I was able to have insulation blown into the floor joist bays, solving the heat problem in all but the lower-level bedroom. Here is another instance where I should have followed my instincts: I had considered insulating the bedroom ceiling with foam boards between the strapping. Quilted shades were also added to reduce night-time heat loss through the glass windows and doors.

The first hard freeze of the second winter froze the bathroom water pipe. I knew there were two pipes within inches of each other and could not understand why only one pipe froze. I was able to get at the pipes by removing one of the soffit boards, but all that revealed was that everything was okay. I finally cut a hole in the wall in back of the sink cabinet and there it was, a $\frac{1}{4}$-in. section of pipe was not covered with foam. The exposed gap was at the top of the subfloor (not visible from the soffit outside) and it happened to be where the cold travels. I was lucky to find this problem before the pipe burst. The pipe is now covered and there has been no more freezing problem.

The second summer was when one plastic jug in the heatbox leaked. I could not take a chance that it was just a defective jug, so out all the jugs came. My system for removing these soft plastic jugs, which had no handles, was to grab the upper corners of each one and carry it, in a hunchbacked position, over to the attic access opening, squat to my knees and gently lower it to my wife who was standing on a stepladder below. The first half-filled jug was a piece of cake. The second one was also easy. It went directly from the attic to the garage floor. We finally got the system down pat except I kept skinning my knuckles. I don't know what was worse, my knuckles or the heat. My wife had an equally good time with her part of removing those thirty jugs.

If I were to build this house again, I would install an insulated stud wall along the inside face and spaced 3 in. from the north concrete wall instead of insulating the outside. You lose 6 in. in the rooms, but it makes work much easier for plumbing and wiring. It's cheaper, and just as effective. Air-lock entrances at the lower-level doors would also have been a nice addition.

A wood stove was finally added in October of 1984, and a good addition it is. The early results are very pleasing to Betty, but it really needs a complete winter to find out how much wood it takes to keep the house comfortable. No replacement was made for the water jugs. Betty will try it with just air and no heat storage for the winter of 1985.

A Note from Betty Price

On the whole, my house is wonderful—nearly all I had hoped for when I decided to build a solar house. It is tight and well insulated, and on sunny winter days it is warm—even hot. Conversely, it is cool in the summer and has excellent cross-ventilation. I love my upstairs storage room. It is much better than a dark, spidery basement. And with no windows on the front of the house, I am unaware of the street noises.

If I were doing it over, I don't think I would choose radiant heat. It is very slow to warm the rooms on dark winter days. Now that I have a wood stove, I probably won't have to use it. The brick floor is beautiful and is warm on sunny days, but cold on cloudy ones. And having no windows on the front is also a minus: I have no way of knowing who is ringing the doorbell.

However, I wouldn't trade my house for anything. The longer I live in it, the better I like it.

Editor: Laura Cehanowicz Tringali
Design Director: Roger Barnes
Associate Editor: Scott Landis
Associate Art Director: C. Heather B. Lambert
Copy/Production Editor: Nancy Stabile
Copy Editor: Ceila Robbins
Layout Artist: Lisa Long
Manager of Production Services: Gary Mancini
Coordinator of Production Services: Dave DeFeo
Production Manager: Mary Galpin
System Operator: Claudia Blake Applegate
Darkroom: Deborah Cooper
Typeface: ITC Garamond
Paper: Hammermill South Shore Offset, 80 lb.
Printer and Binder: The Maple-Vail Book Manufacturing Group, Binghamton, N.Y.